CD INCLUDED

HAL•LEONARD

BIG BAND PLAY-ALONG

VOLUME 5

PIANO

Christmas Favorites

T0078922

ISBN 978-1-4234-5854-8

HAL•LEONARD®
CORPORATION
7777 W. BLUEMOUND RD. P.O. BOX 13819 MILWAUKEE, WI 53213

HAL•LEONARD BIG BAND PLAY-ALONG VOLUME 5

CD INCLUDED

Christmas Favorites

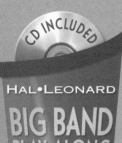

From the Motion Picture **NEPTUNE'S DAUGHTER**

BABY, IT'S COLD OUTSIDE

PIANO

By FRANK LOESSER
Arranged by ROGER HOLMES

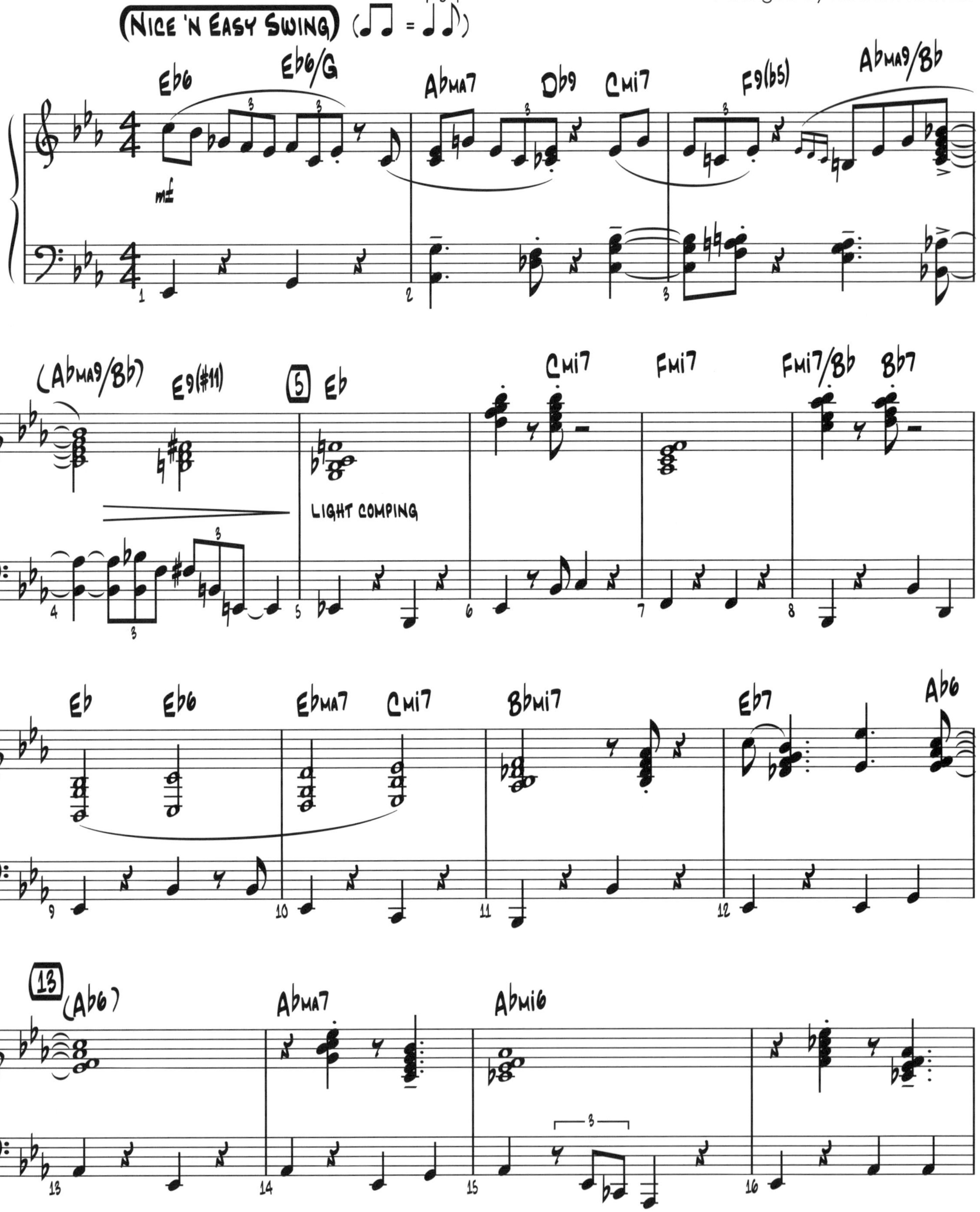

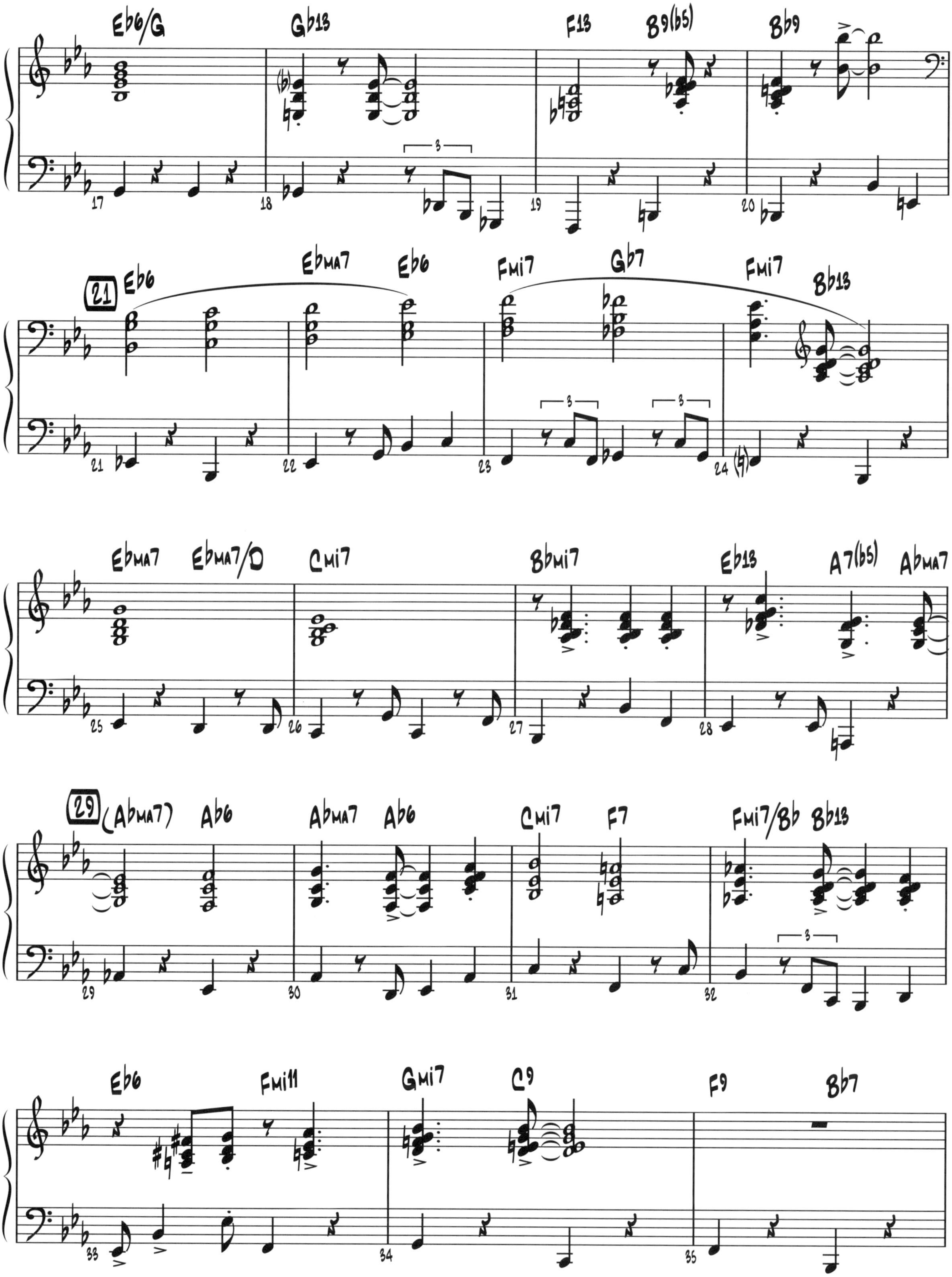
Eb6/G
Gb13
F13
B9(b5)
Bb9
21
Eb6
EbMA7
Eb6
FMI7
Gb7
FMI7
Bb13
EbMA7
EbMA7/D
CMI7
BbMI7
Eb13
A7(b5)
AbMA7
29
(AbMA7)
Ab6
AbMA7
Ab6
CMI7
F7
FMI7/Bb
Bb13
Eb6
FMI11
GMI7
C9
F9
Bb7

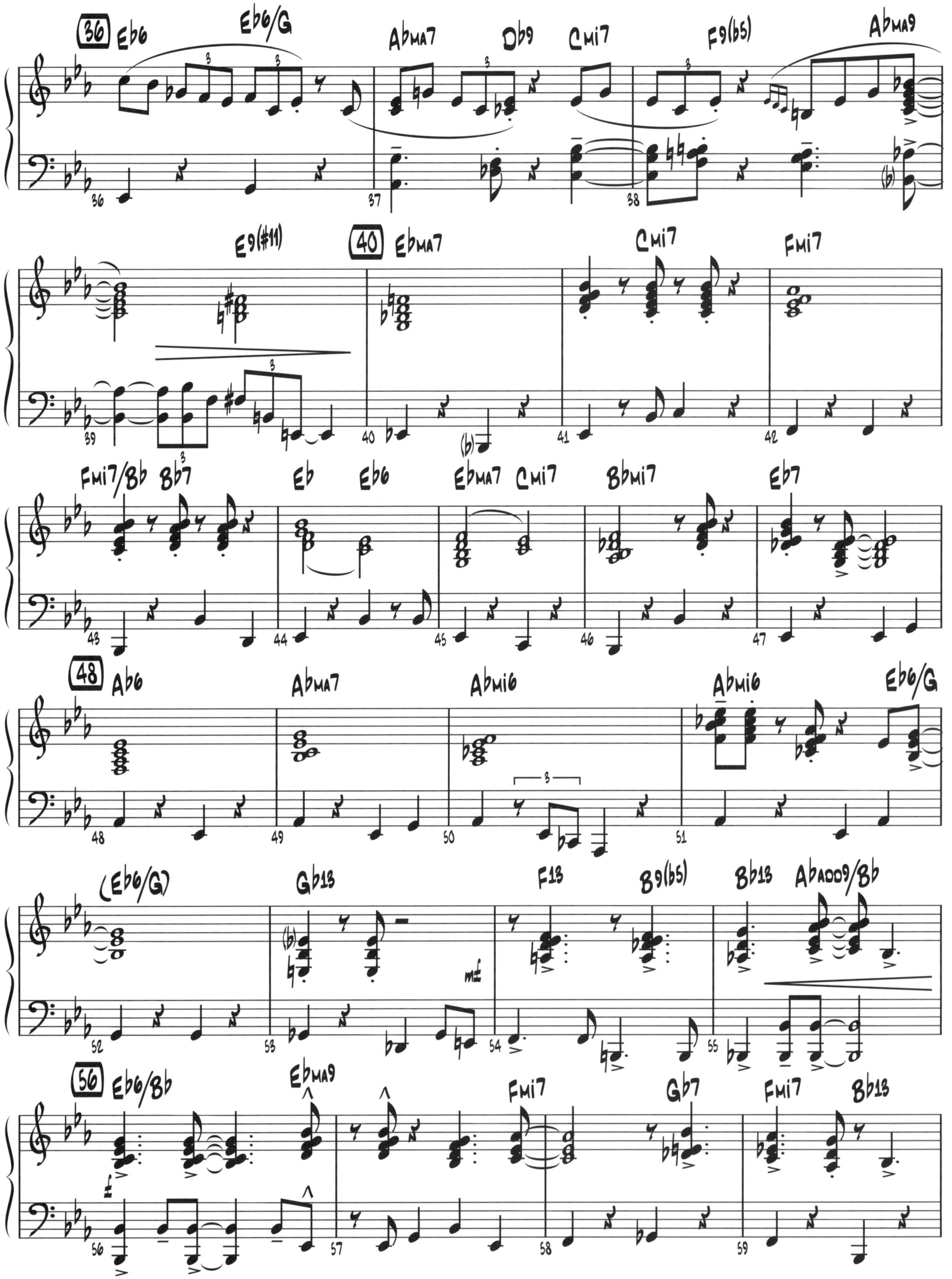
36
Eb6
Eb6/G
Abma7
Db9
Cmi7
F9(b5)
Abma9
E9(#11)
40
Ebma7
Cmi7
Fmi7
Fmi7/Bb
Bb7
Eb
Eb6
Ebma7
Cmi7
Bbmi7
Eb7
48
Ab6
Abma7
Abmi6
Abmi6
Eb6/G
(Eb6/G)
Gb13
mf
F13
B9(b5)
Bb13
Abadd9/Bb
56
Eb6/Bb
f
Ebma9
Fmi7
Gb7
Fmi7
Bb13

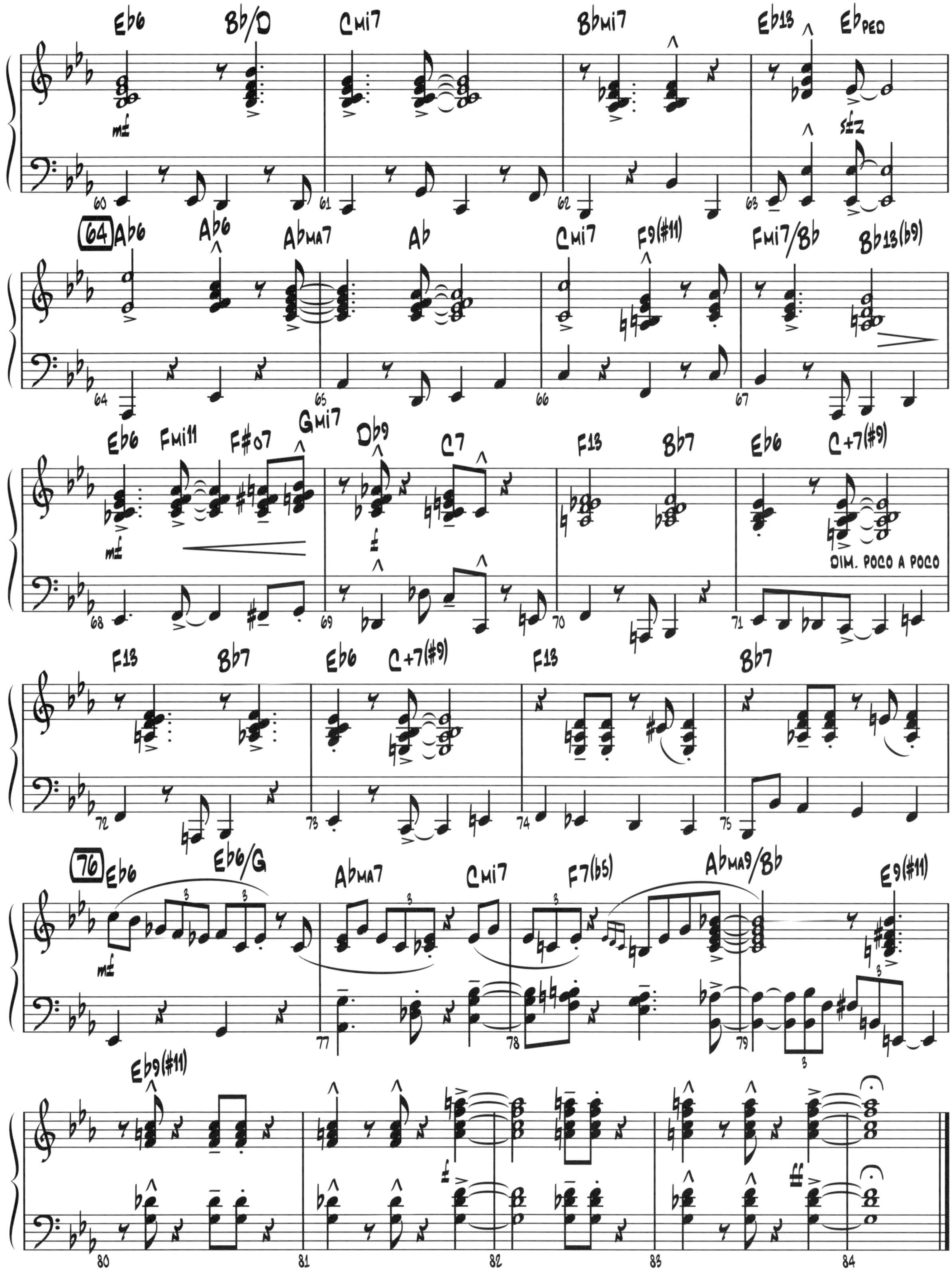
Eb6 Bb/D Cmi7 Bbmi7 Eb13 Ebped
mf
sfz
60 61 62 63
64 Ab6 Ab6 Abma7 Ab Cmi7 F9(#11) Fmi7/Bb Bb13(b9)
64 65 66 67
Eb6 Fmi11 F#o7 Gmi7 Db9 C7 F13 Bb7 Eb6 C+7(#9)
mf
f
DIM. POCO A POCO
68 69 70 71
F13 Bb7 Eb6 C+7(#9) F13 Bb7
72 73 74 75
76 Eb6 Eb6/G Abma7 Cmi7 F7(b5) Abma9/Bb E9(#11)
mf
77 78 79
Eb9(#11)
f
ff
80 81 82 83 84

THIS PAGE HAS BEEN LEFT BLANK TO ACCOMMODATE PAGE TURNS.

THE CHRISTMAS SONG
(CHESTNUTS ROASTING ON AN OPEN FIRE)

Music and Lyric by
MEL TORME and ROBERT WELLS
Arranged by PAUL JENNINGS

PIANO

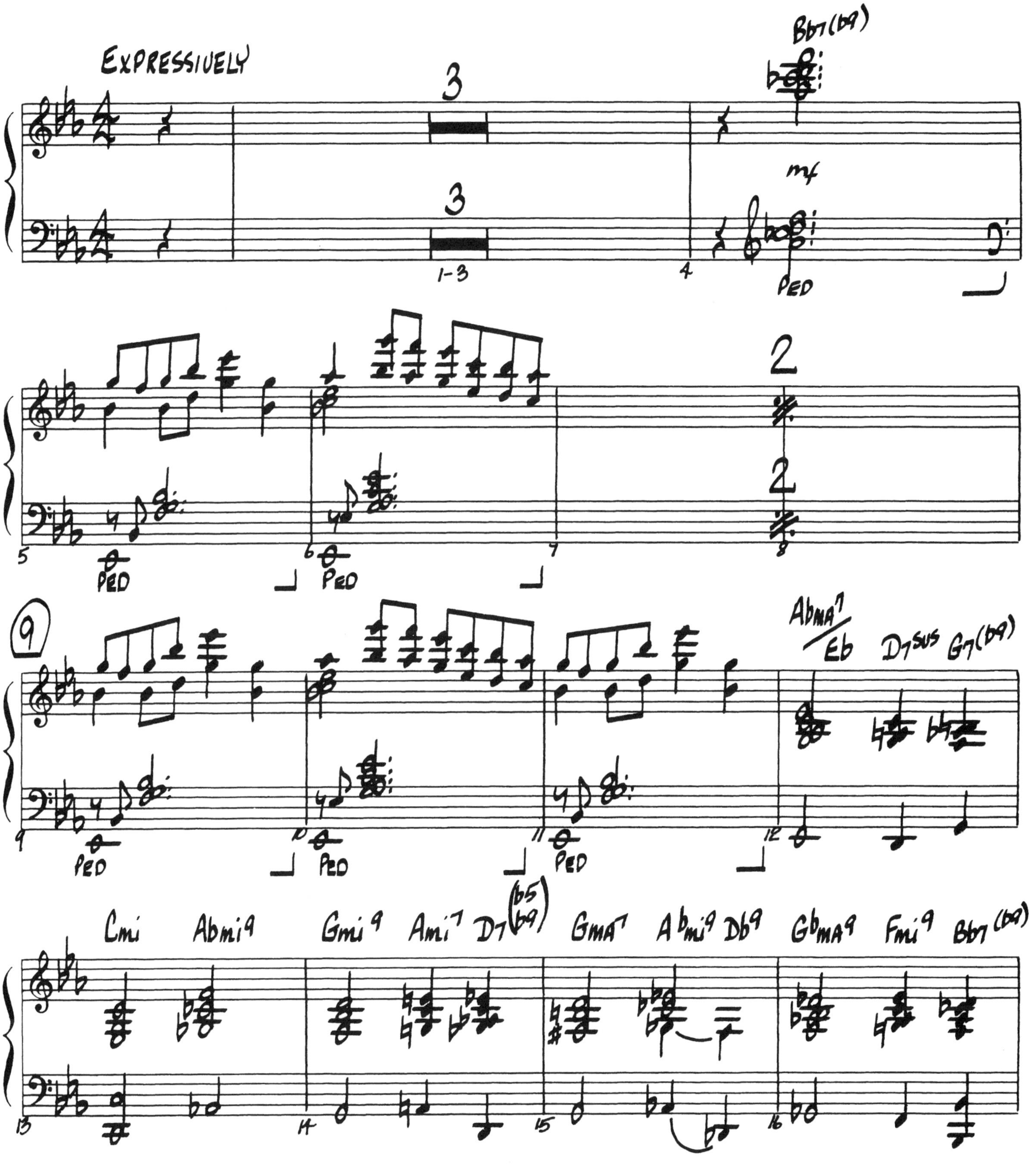

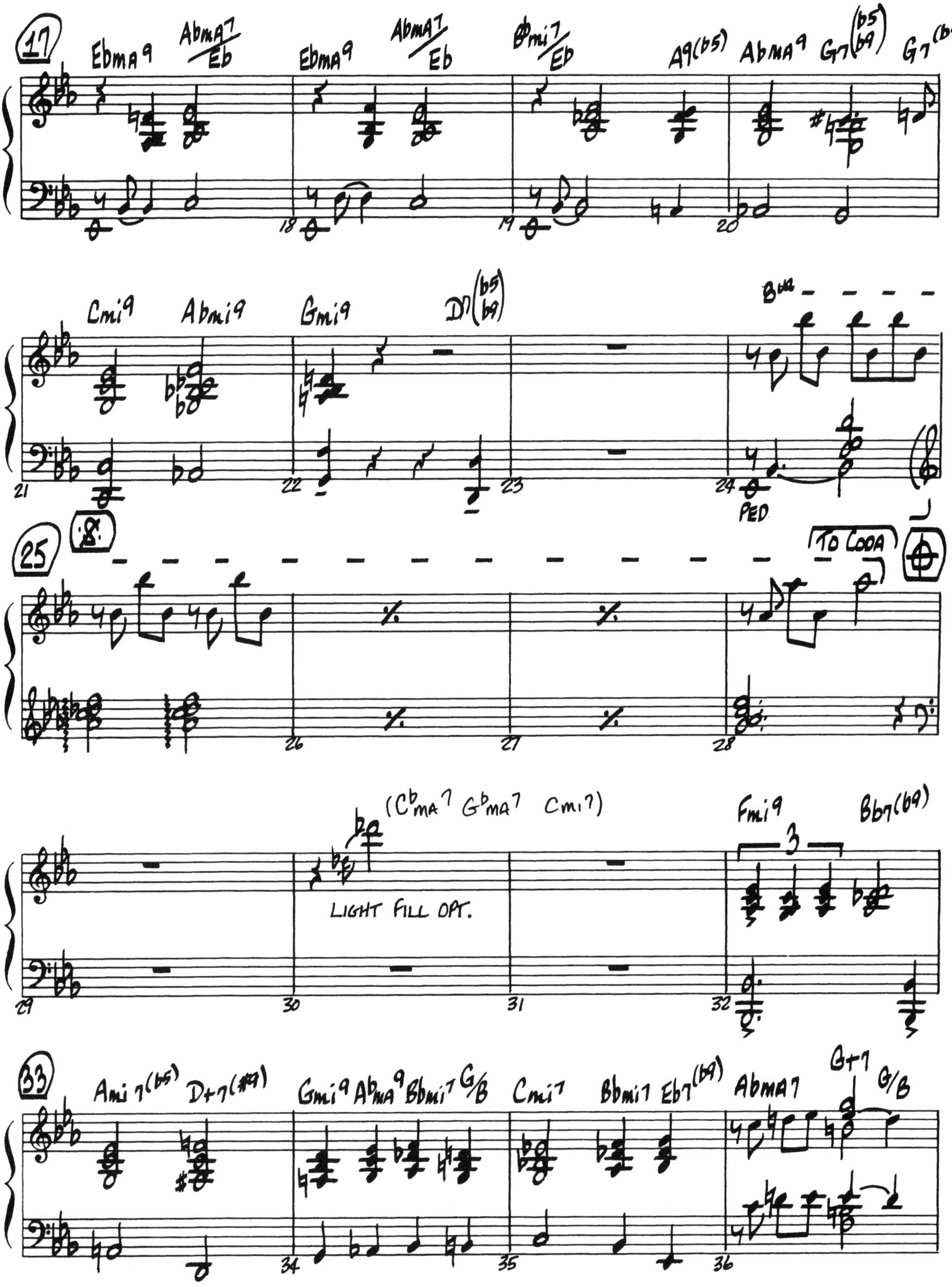
17
Ebma9
Abma7/Eb
Ebma9
Abma7/Eb
Bbmi7/Eb
A9(b5)
Abma9
G7(b5 b9)
G7(b9)
Cmi9
Abmi9
Gmi9
D7(b5 b9)
8va
PED
25
TO CODA
(Cbma7 Gbma7 Cmi7)
LIGHT FILL OPT.
Fmi9
Bb7(b9)
33
Ami7(b5)
D+7(#9)
Gmi9
Abma9
Bbmi7
G/B
Cmi7
Bbmi7
Eb7(b9)
Abma7
G+7
G/B

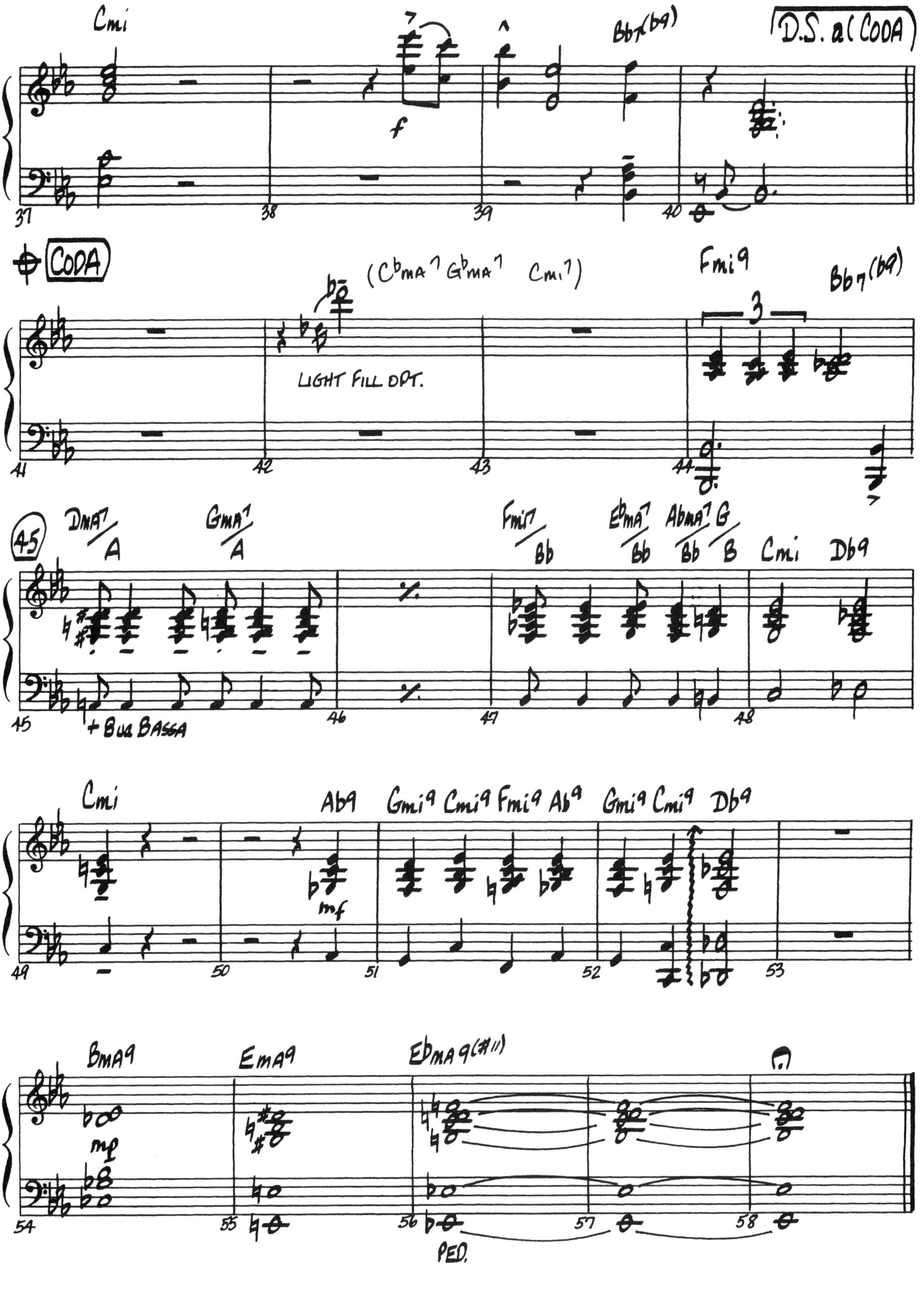
Cmi
Bb7(b9)
D.S. al CODA
f
CODA
(Cbma7 Gbma7 Cmi7)
Fmi9
Bb7(b9)
LIGHT FILL OPT.
45
Dma7/A
Gma7/A
Fmi7/Bb
Ebma7/Bb
Abma7/Bb
G/B
Cmi
Db9
+ Bua BASSA
Cmi
Ab9
Gmi9 Cmi9 Fmi9 Ab9
Gmi9 Cmi9
Db9
mf
Bma9
Ema9
Ebma9(#11)
mp
PED.

FELIZ NAVIDAD

PIANO

Music and Lyrics by
JOSE FELICIANO
Arranged by PAUL MURTHA

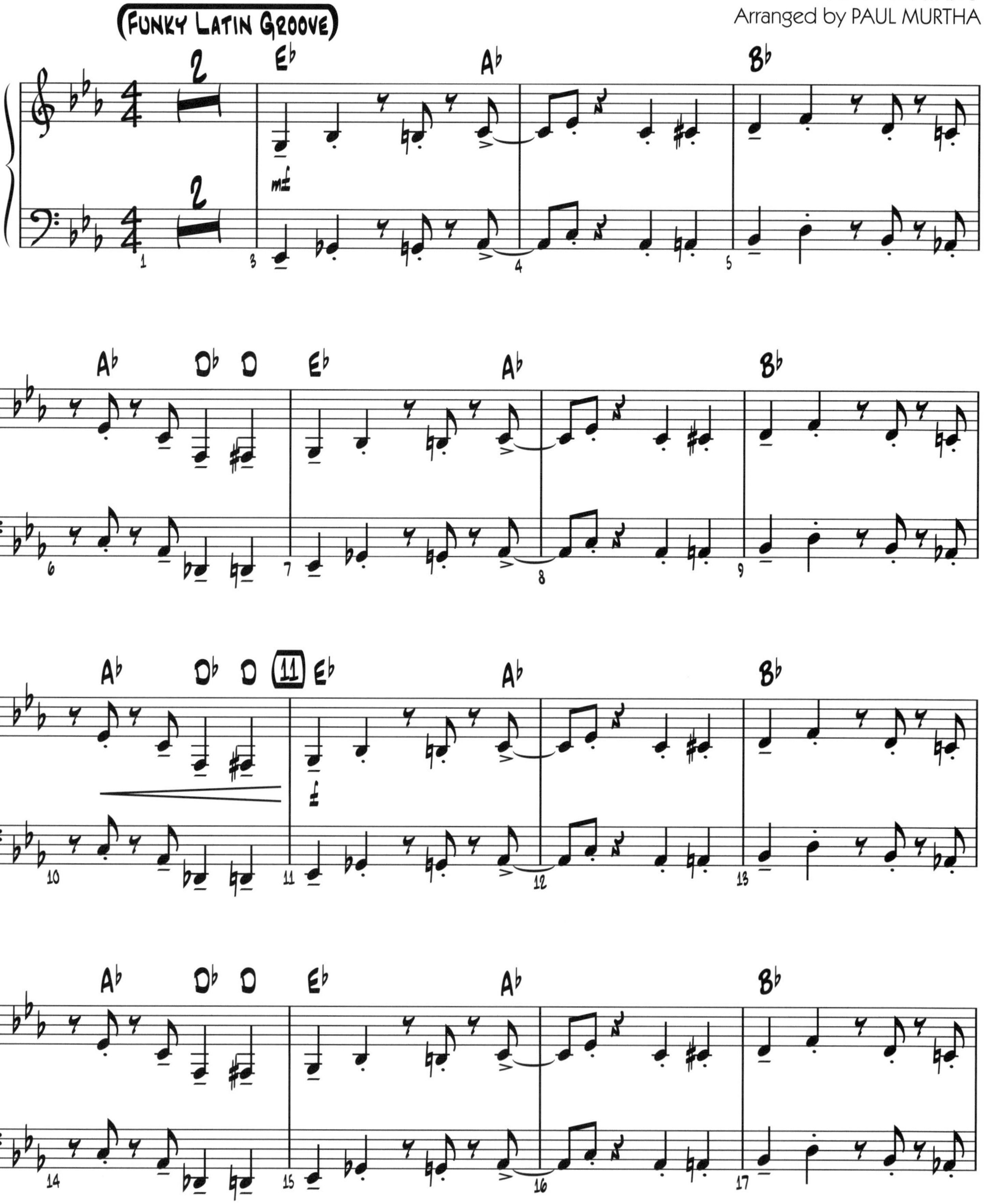

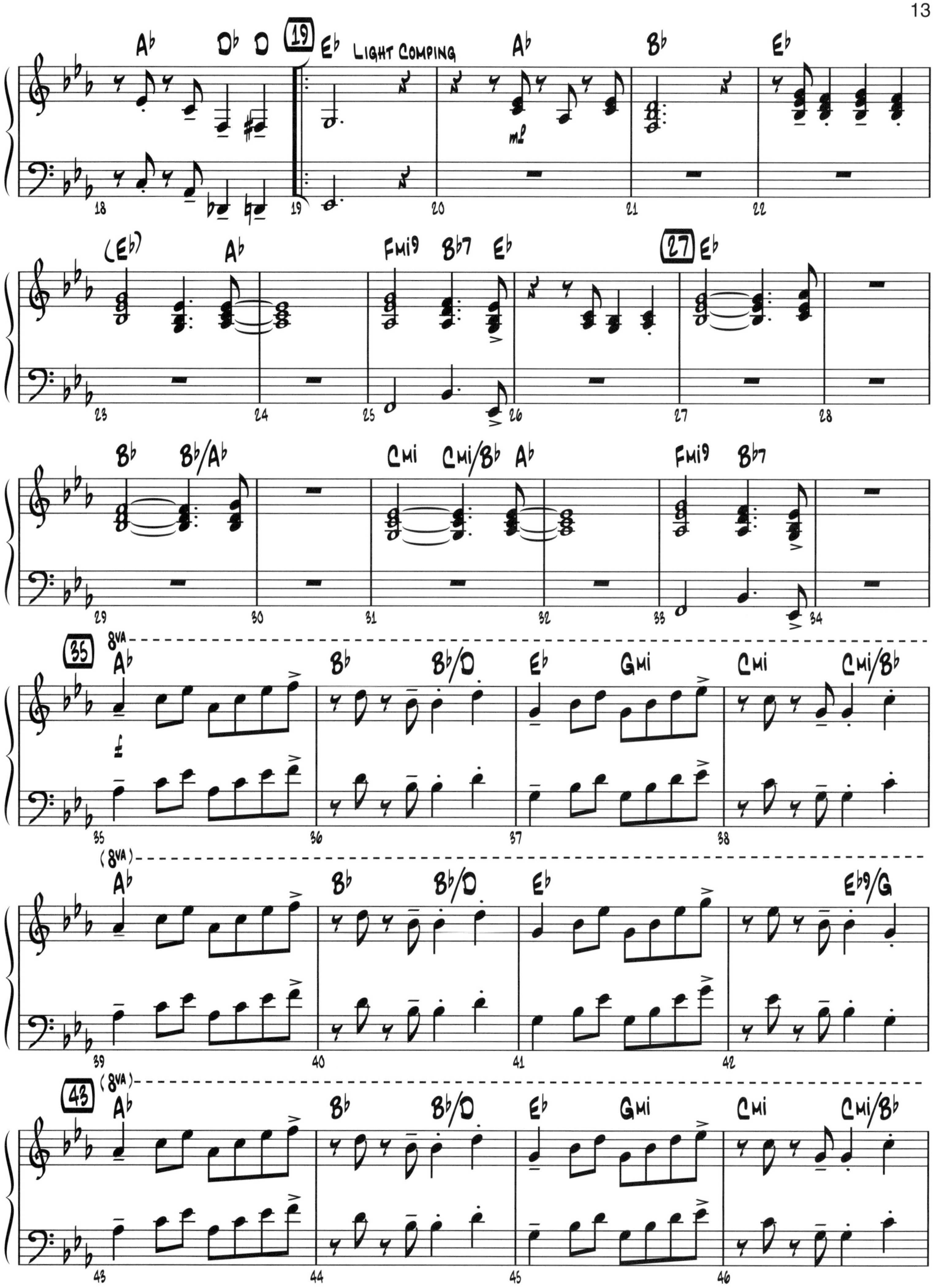
Ab Db D
19
Eb Light Comping
Ab
Bb
Eb
mf
(Eb) Ab
FMI9 Bb7 Eb
27
Eb
Bb Bb/Ab
CMI CMI/Bb Ab
FMI9 Bb7
35
8VA
Ab Bb Bb/D Eb GMI CMI CMI/Bb
f
(8VA)
Ab Bb Bb/D Eb Eb9/G
43
(8VA)
Ab Bb Bb/D Eb GMI CMI CMI/Bb

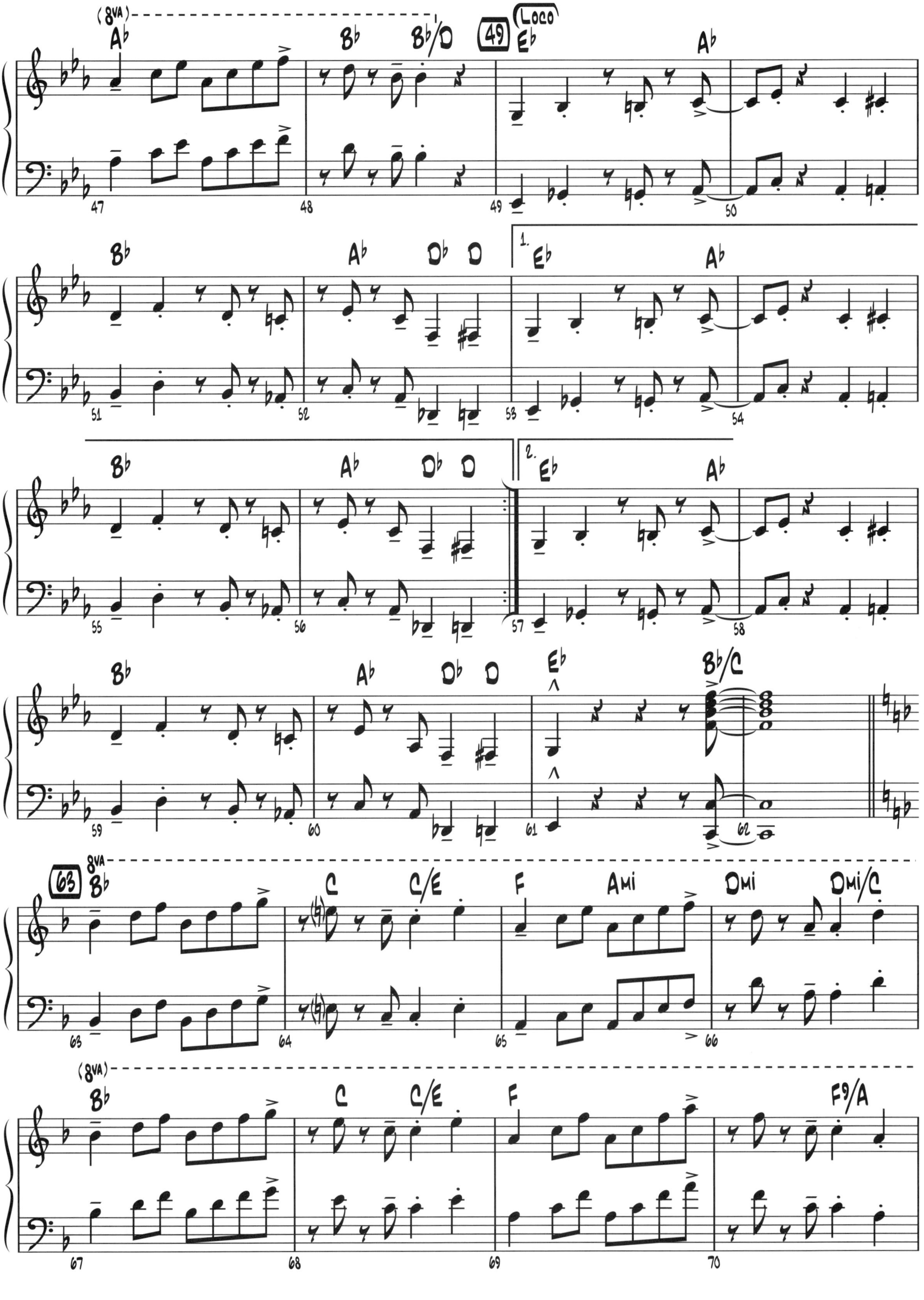
(8VA)
Ab
Bb
Bb/D
49
(Loco
Eb
Ab
Bb
Ab
Db
D
1.
Eb
Ab
Bb
Ab
Db
D
2.
Eb
Ab
Bb
Ab
Db
D
Eb
Bb/C
63
8VA
Bb
C
C/E
F
AMI
DMI
DMI/C
(8VA)
Bb
C
C/E
F
F9/A

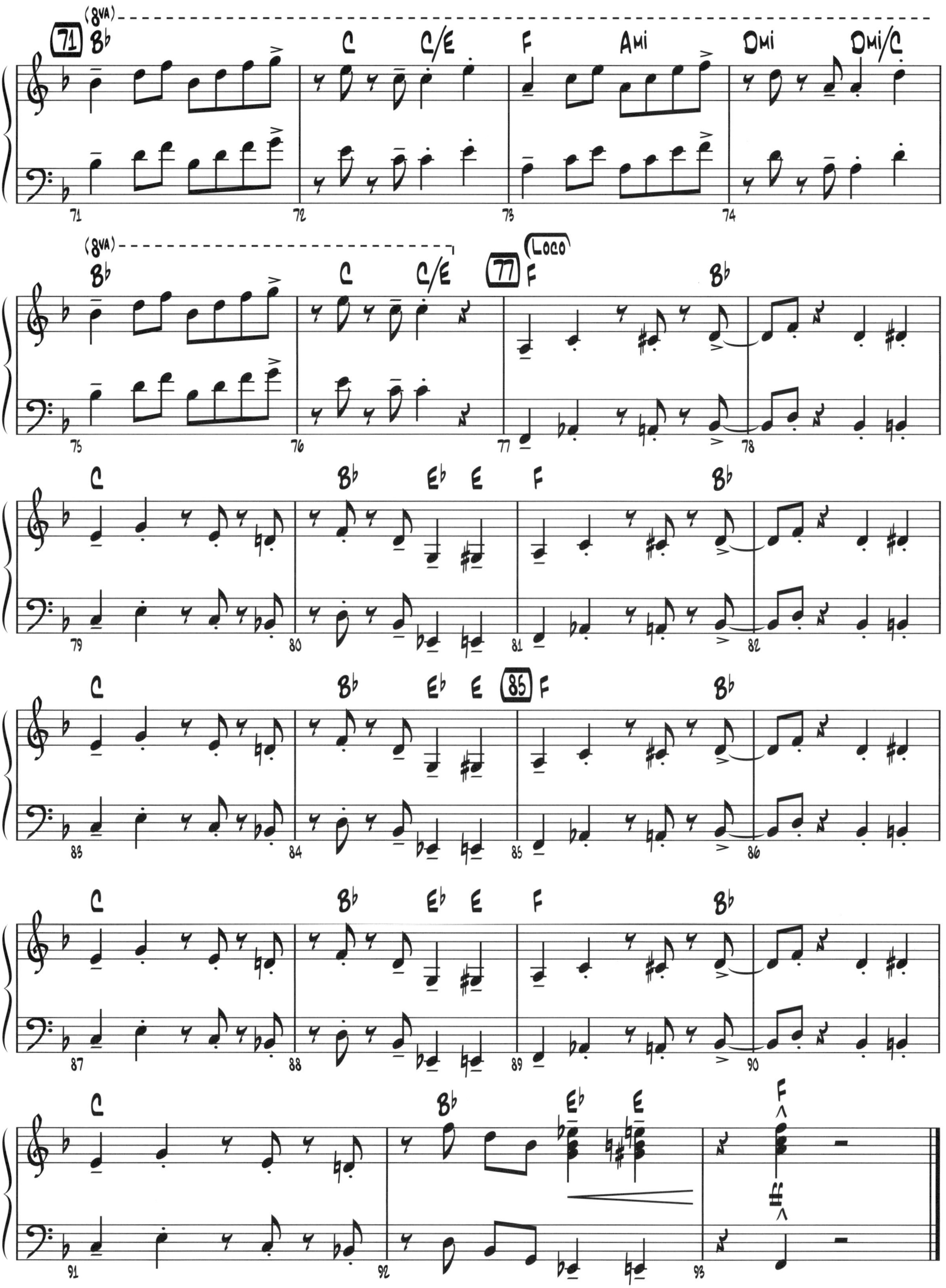
(8VA)
71
B♭ C C/E F AMI DMI DMI/C
71 72 73 74
(8VA)
B♭ C C/E
77
(LOCO)
F B♭
75 76 77 78
C B♭ E♭ E F B♭
79 80 81 82
C B♭ E♭ E
85
F B♭
83 84 85 86
C B♭ E♭ E F B♭
87 88 89 90
C B♭ E♭ E F
ff
91 92 93

I'LL BE HOME FOR CHRISTMAS

PIANO

Words and Music by
KIM GANNON and WALTER KENT
Arranged by JOHN BERRY

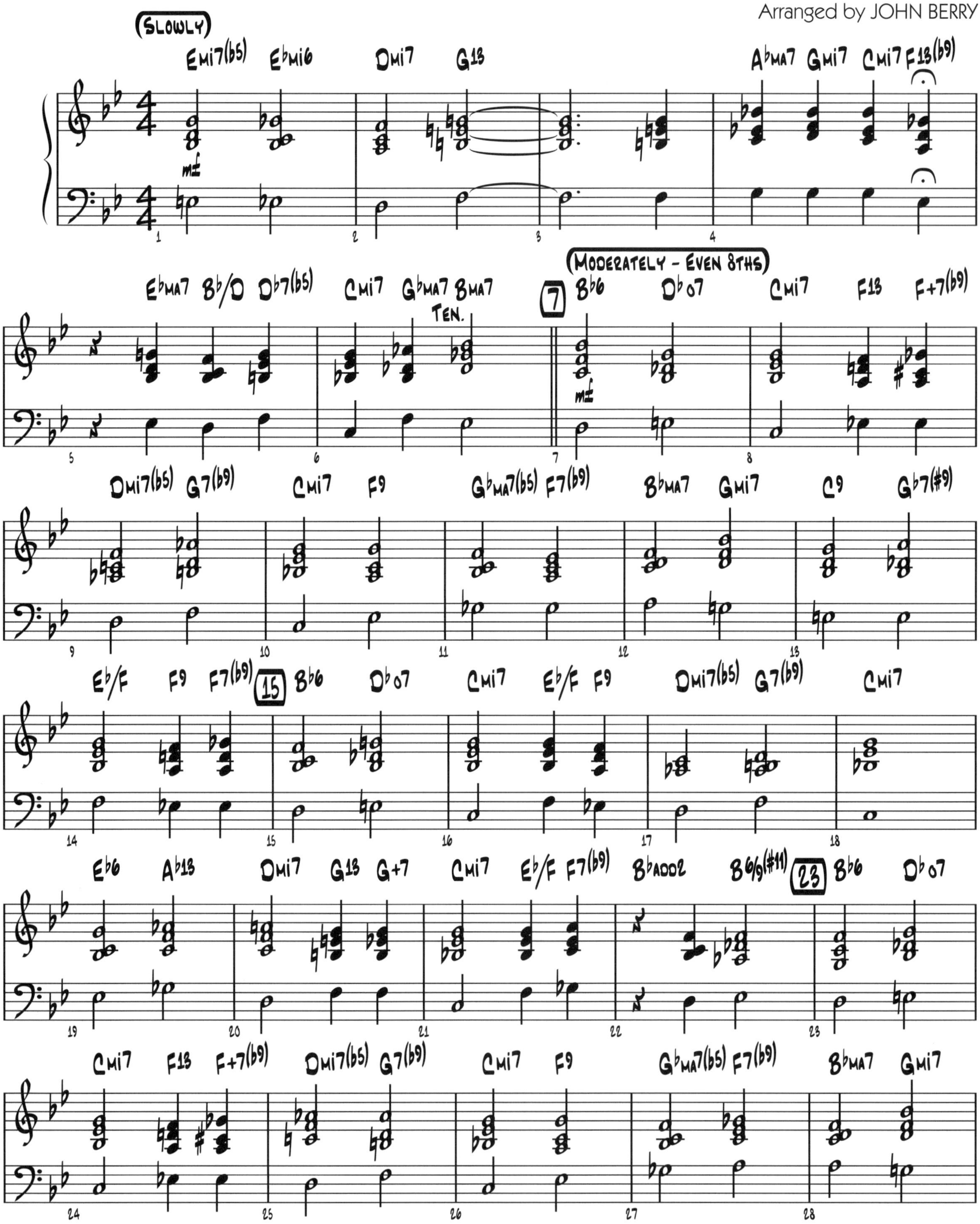

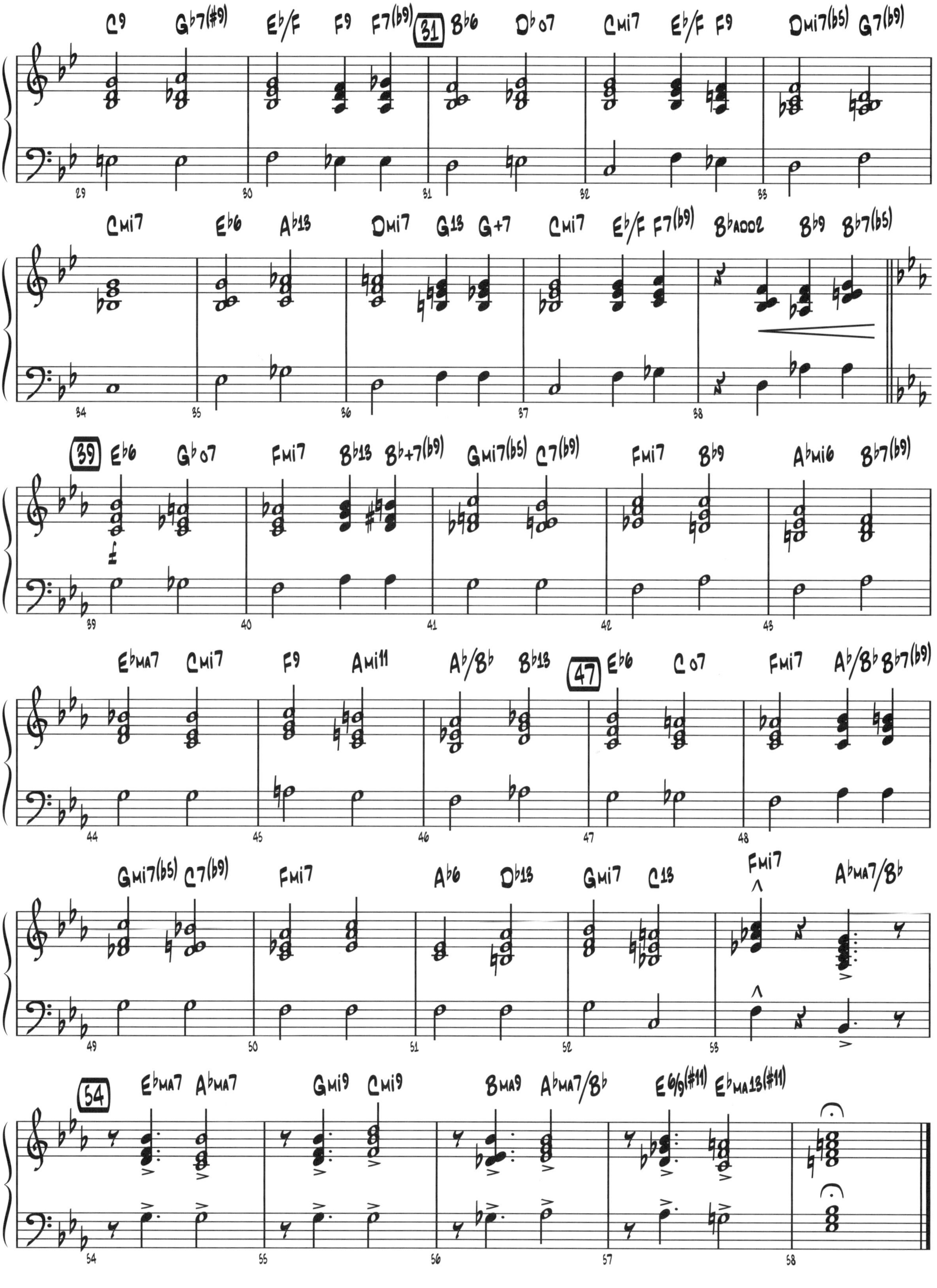
C9 G♭7(#9) E♭/F F9 F7(♭9) 31 B♭6 D♭°7 CMI7 E♭/F F9 DMI7(♭5) G7(♭9)
CMI7 E♭6 A♭13 DMI7 G13 G+7 CMI7 E♭/F F7(♭9) B♭ADD2 B♭9 B♭7(♭5)
39 E♭6 G♭°7 FMI7 B♭13 B♭+7(♭9) GMI7(♭5) C7(♭9) FMI7 B♭9 A♭MI6 B♭7(♭9)
E♭MA7 CMI7 F9 AMI11 A♭/B♭ B♭13 47 E♭6 C°7 FMI7 A♭/B♭ B♭7(♭9)
GMI7(♭5) C7(♭9) FMI7 A♭6 D♭13 GMI7 C13 FMI7 A♭MA7/B♭
54 E♭MA7 A♭MA7 GMI9 CMI9 BMA9 A♭MA7/B♭ E6/9(#11) E♭MA13(#11)

LET IT SNOW! LET IT SNOW! LET IT SNOW!

Words by SAMMY CAHN
Music by JULE STYNE
Arranged by PAUL LAVENDER

PIANO

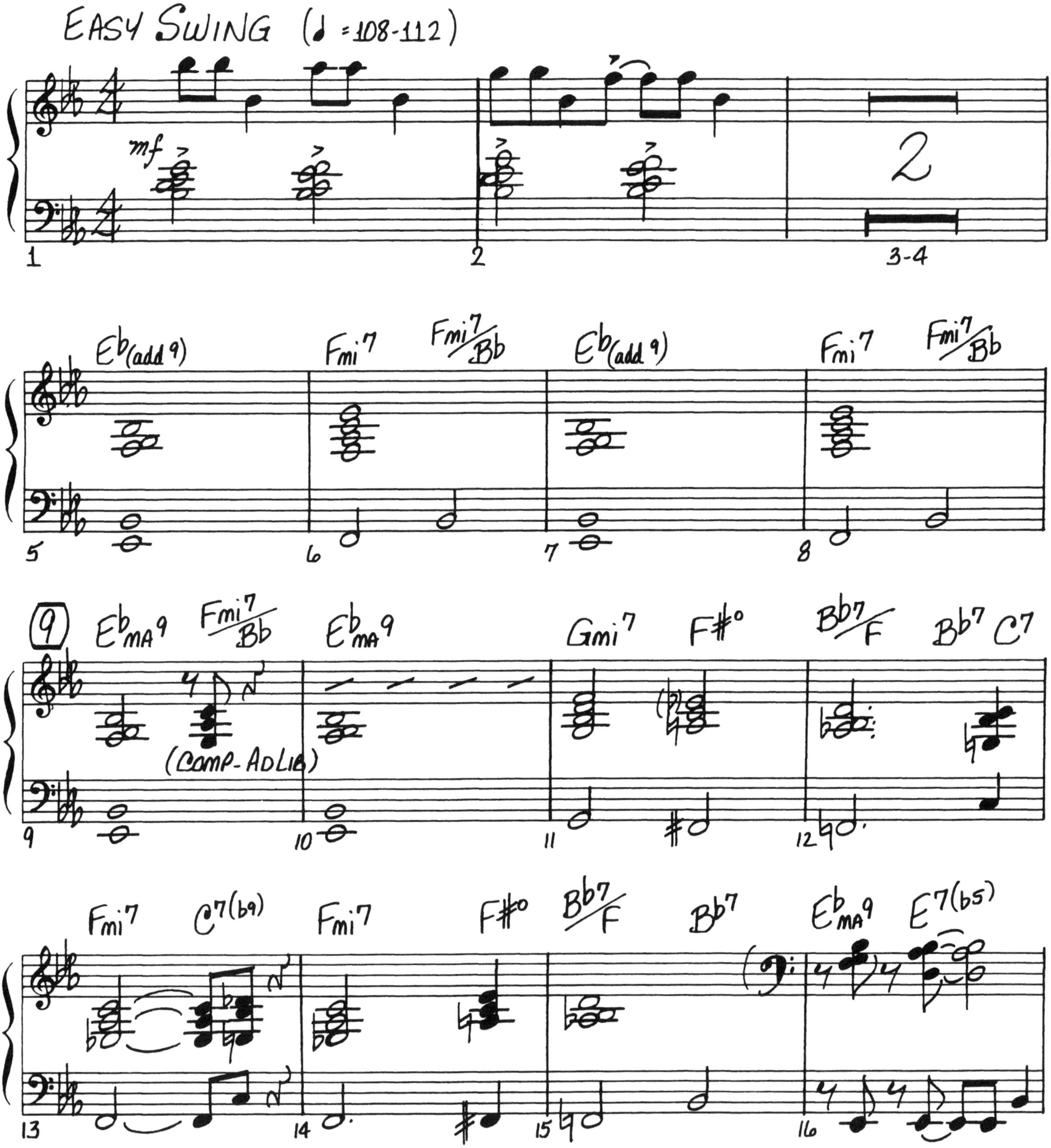

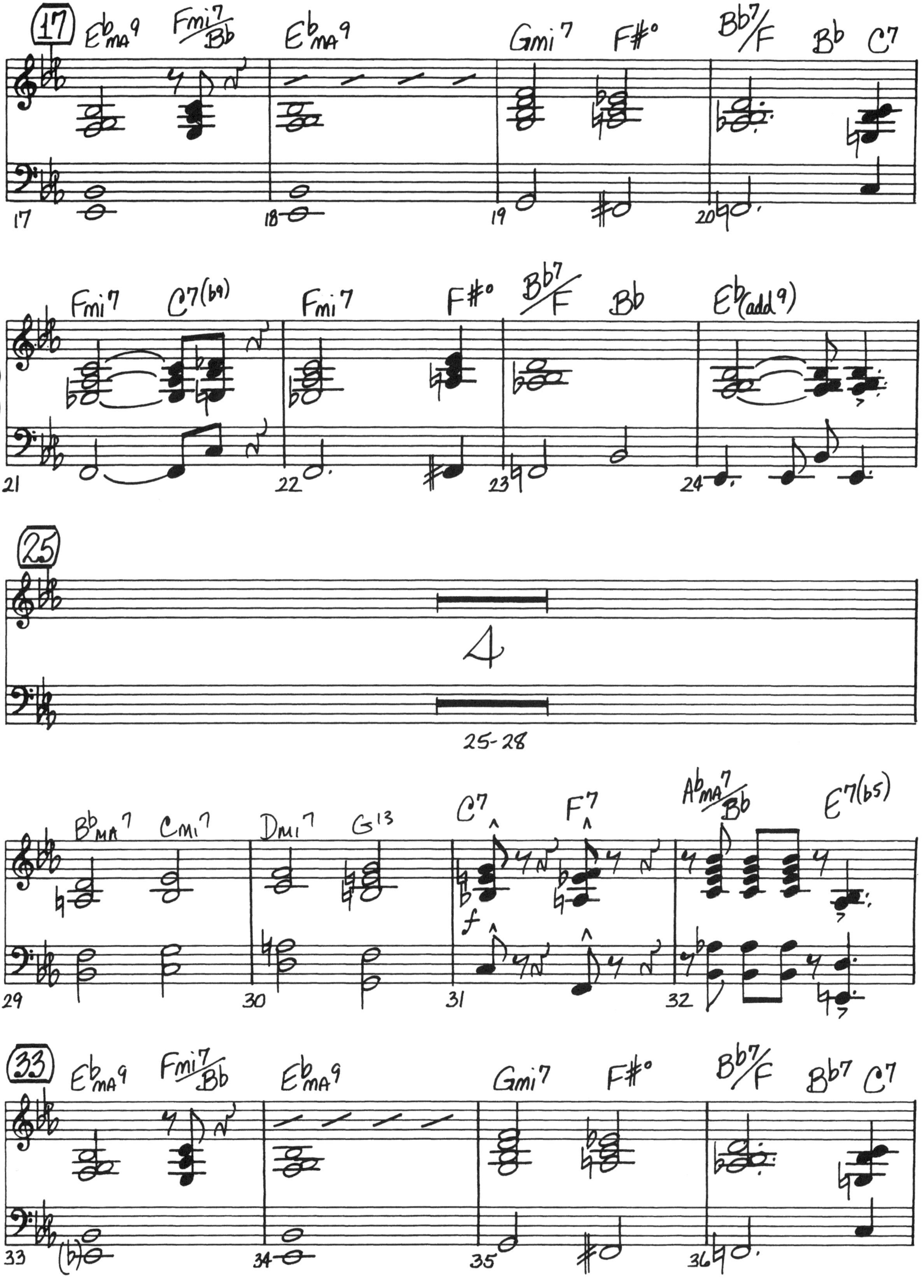
17
Ebma9 Fmi7/Bb Ebma9 Gmi7 F#° Bb7/F Bb C7
Fmi7 C7(b9) Fmi7 F#° Bb7/F Bb Eb(add9)
25
4
25-28
Bbma7 Cmi7 Dmi7 G13 C7 F7 Abma7/Bb E7(b5)
f
33
Ebma9 Fmi7/Bb Ebma9 Gmi7 F#° Bb7/F Bb7 C7

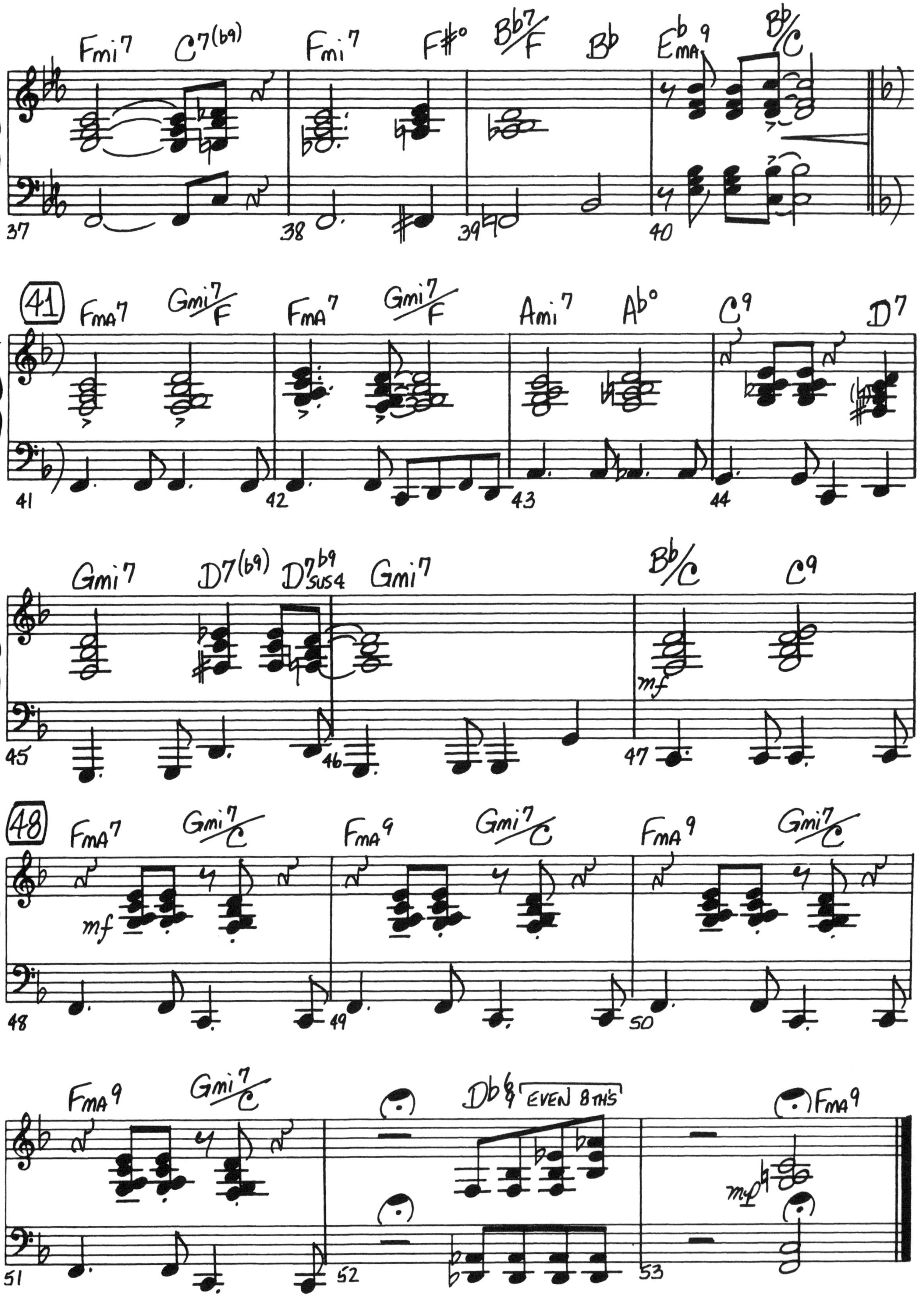
Fmi7 C7(b9) Fmi7 F#° Bb7/F Bb Ebma9 Bb/C
37 38 39 40
41 Fma7 Gmi7/F Fma7 Gmi7/F Ami7 Ab° C9 D7
41 42 43 44
Gmi7 D7(b9) D7b9sus4 Gmi7 Bb/C C9
mf
45 46 47
48 Fma7 Gmi7/C Fma9 Gmi7/C Fma9 Gmi7/C
mf
48 49 50
Fma9 Gmi7/C Db6/9 EVEN 8TH'S Fma9
mp
51 52 53

LITTLE SAINT NICK

Words and Music by
BRIAN WILSON and MIKE LOVE
Arranged by JOHN BERRY

PIANO

(SWING)

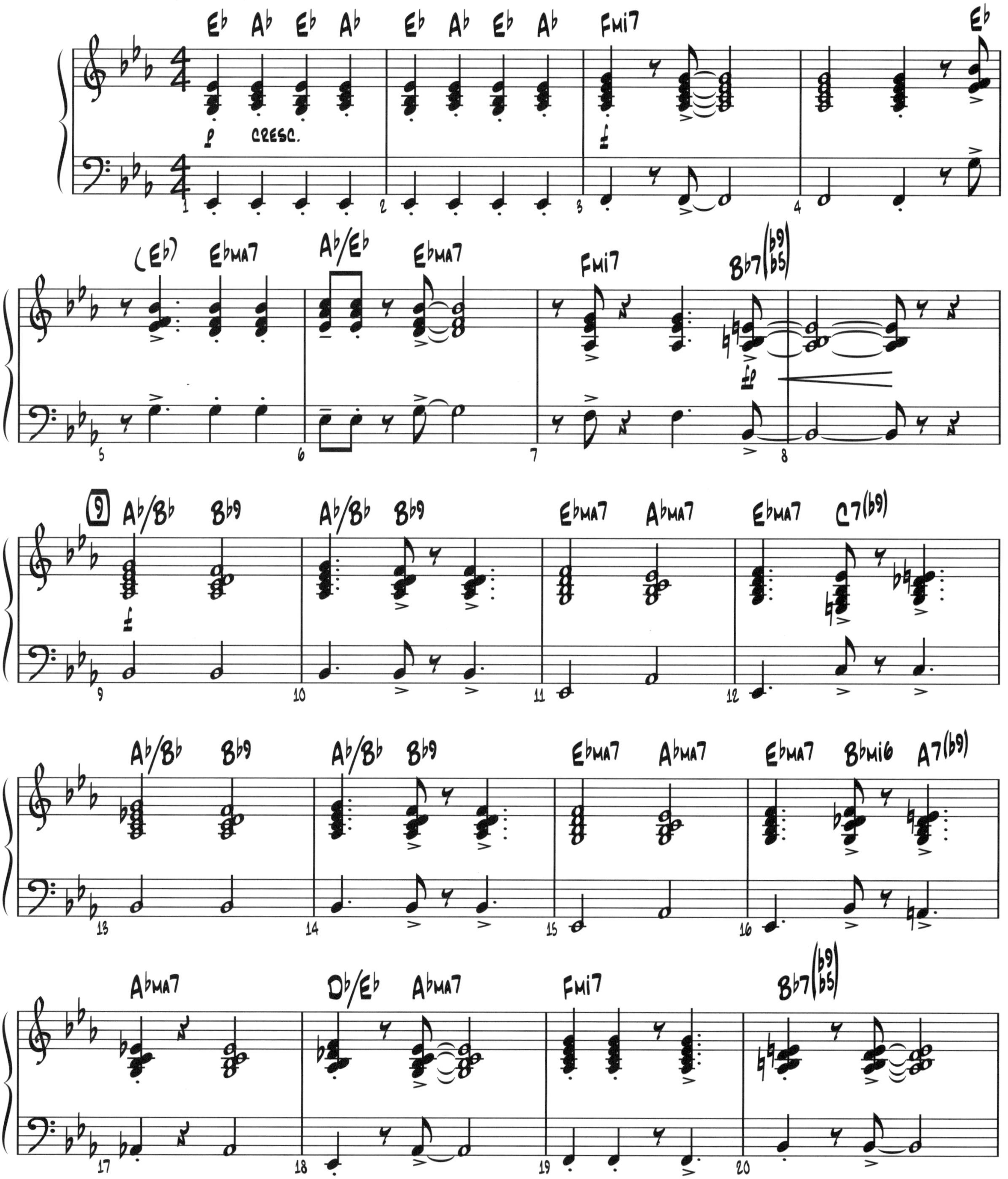

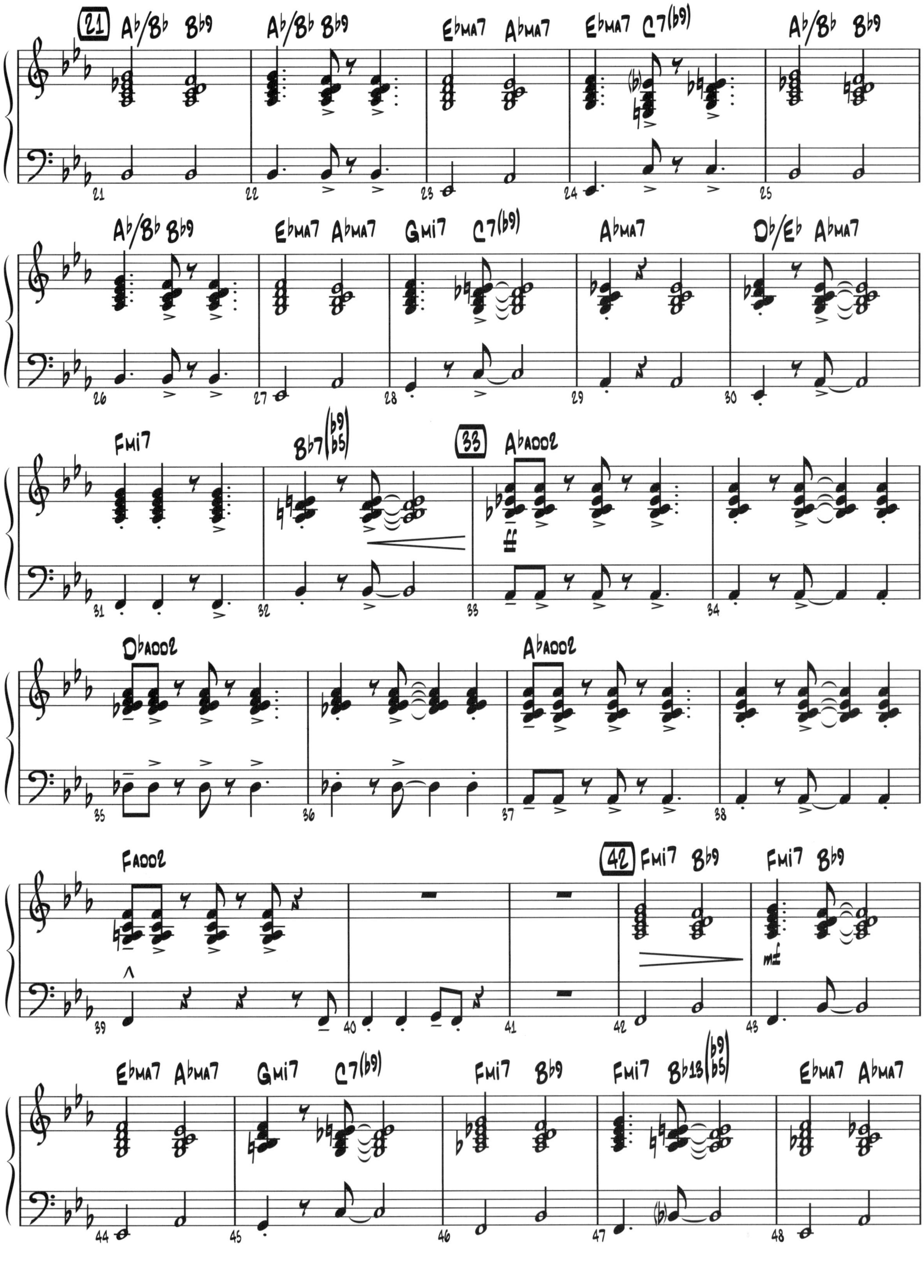
21 Ab/Bb Bb9 Ab/Bb Bb9 Ebma7 Abma7 Ebma7 C7(b9) Ab/Bb Bb9
Ab/Bb Bb9 Ebma7 Abma7 Gmi7 C7(b9) Abma7 Db/Eb Abma7
Fmi7 Bb7(b9 b5) 33 AbADD2
ff
DbADD2 AbADD2
FADD2 42 Fmi7 Bb9 Fmi7 Bb9
mf
Ebma7 Abma7 Gmi7 C7(b9) Fmi7 Bb9 Fmi7 Bb13(b9 b5) Ebma7 Abma7

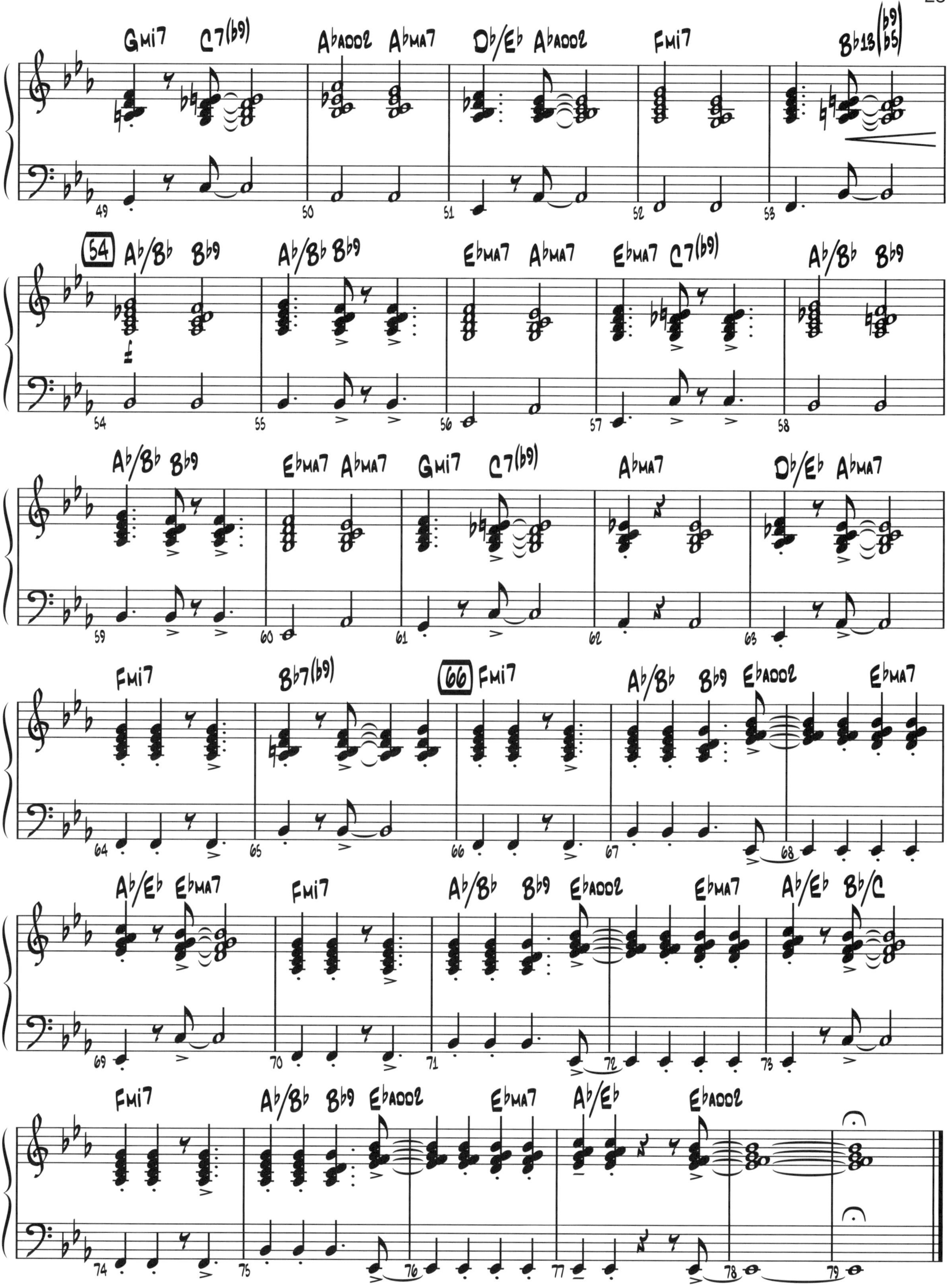
Gmi7 C7(b9) Abadd2 Abma7 Db/Eb Abadd2 Fmi7 Bb13(b9 b5)
54 Ab/Bb Bb9 Ab/Bb Bb9 Ebma7 Abma7 Ebma7 C7(b9) Ab/Bb Bb9
Ab/Bb Bb9 Ebma7 Abma7 Gmi7 C7(b9) Abma7 Db/Eb Abma7
Fmi7 Bb7(b9) 66 Fmi7 Ab/Bb Bb9 Ebadd2 Ebma7
Ab/Eb Ebma7 Fmi7 Ab/Bb Bb9 Ebadd2 Ebma7 Ab/Eb Bb/C
Fmi7 Ab/Bb Bb9 Ebadd2 Ebma7 Ab/Eb Ebadd2

From THE SOUND OF MUSIC

MY FAVORITE THINGS

Lyrics by OSCAR HAMMERSTEIN II
Music by RICHARD RODGERS
Arranged by ROGER HOLMES

PIANO

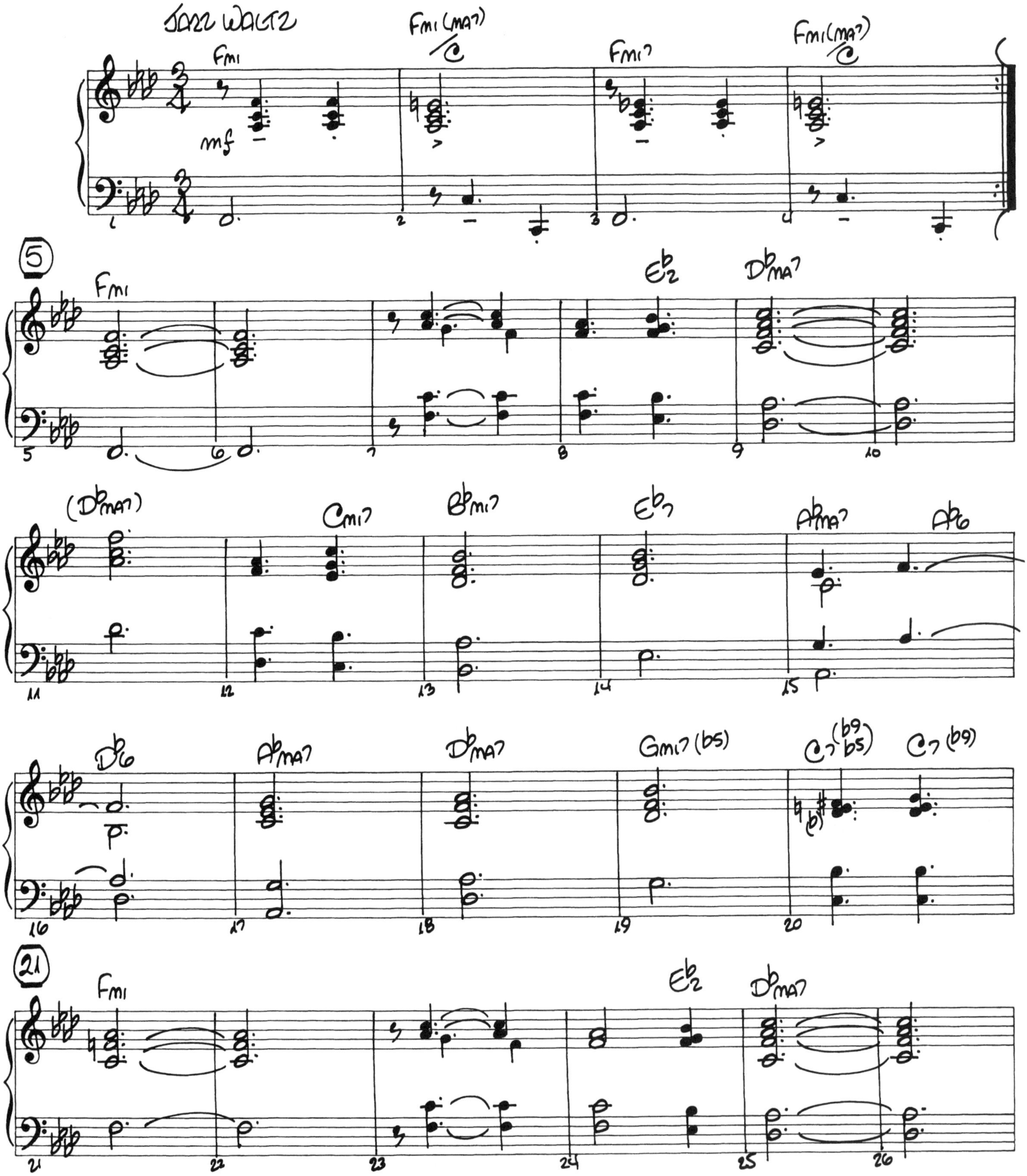

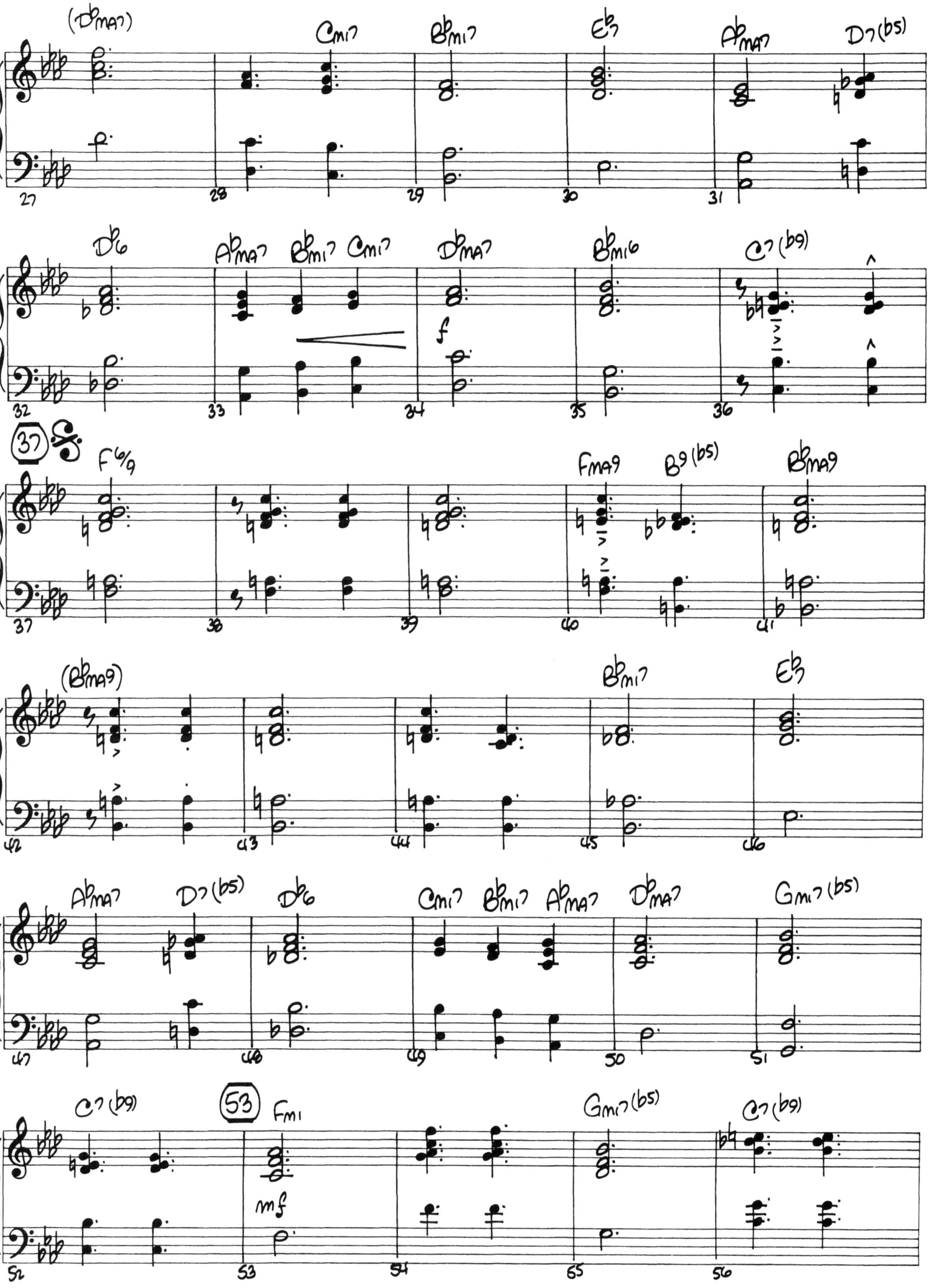
(D♭MA7) Cmi7 B♭mi7 E♭7 A♭MA7 D7(♭5)
27 28 29 30 31
D♭6 A♭MA7 B♭mi7 Cmi7 D♭MA7 B♭mi6 C7(♭9)
f
32 33 34 35 36
37
F6/9 FMA9 B9(♭5) B♭MA9
37 38 39 40 41
(B♭MA9) B♭mi7 E♭7
42 43 44 45 46
A♭MA7 D7(♭5) D♭6 Cmi7 B♭mi7 A♭MA7 D♭MA7 Gmi7(♭5)
47 48 49 50 51
C7(♭9) 53 Fmi Gmi7(♭5) C7(♭9)
mf
52 53 54 55 56

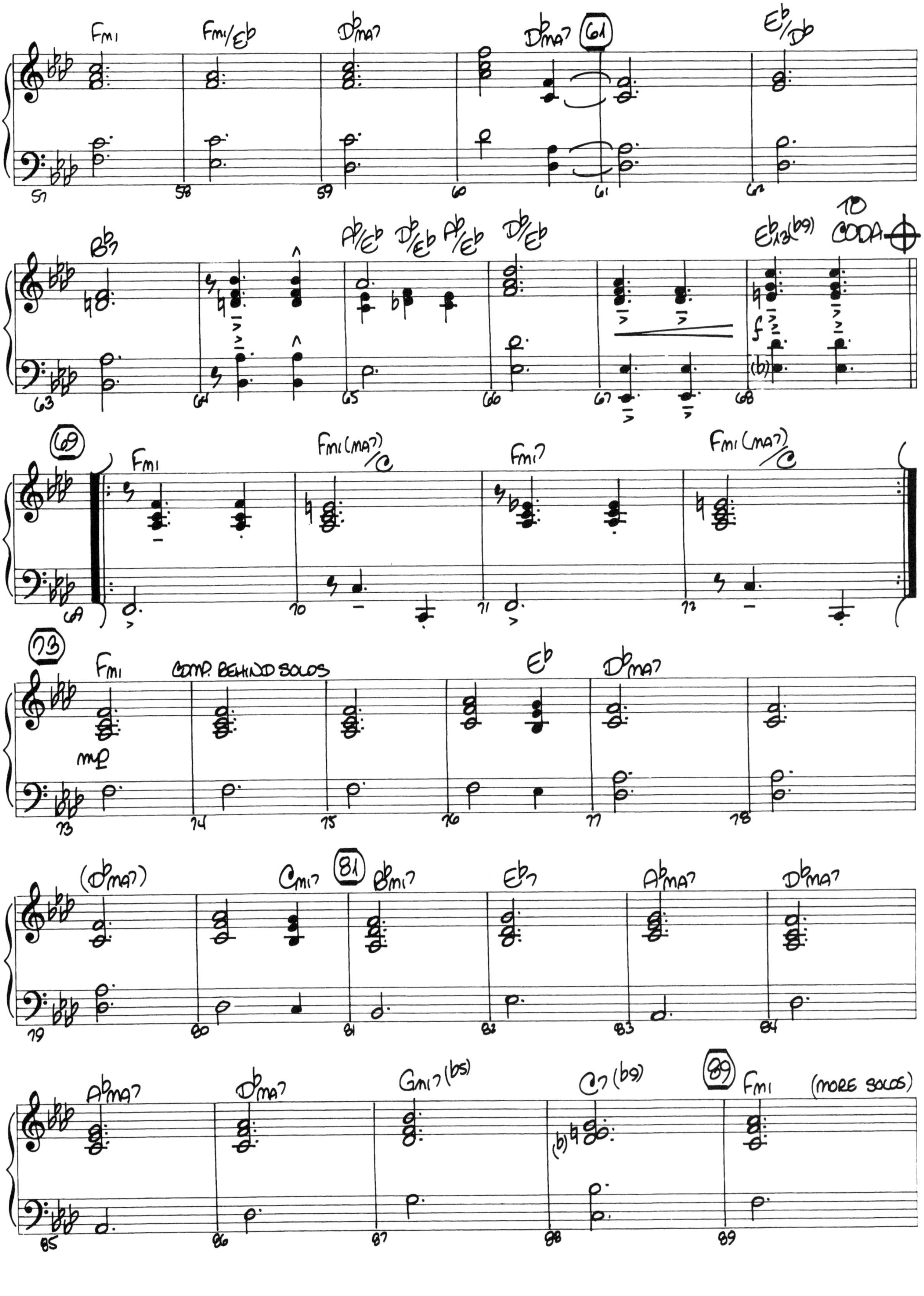
Fmi
Fmi/Eb
Dbma7
Dbma7
61
Eb/Db
Bb7
Ab/Eb
Db/Eb
Ab/Eb
Db/Eb
Eb13(b9)
TO CODA
69
Fmi
Fmi(ma7)/C
Fmi7
Fmi(ma7)/C
73
Fmi
COMP. BEHIND SOLOS
Eb
Dbma7
mp
(Dbma7)
Cmi7
81
Bbmi7
Eb7
Abma7
Dbma7
Abma7
Dbma7
Gmi7(b5)
C7(b9)
89
Fmi
(MORE SOLOS)

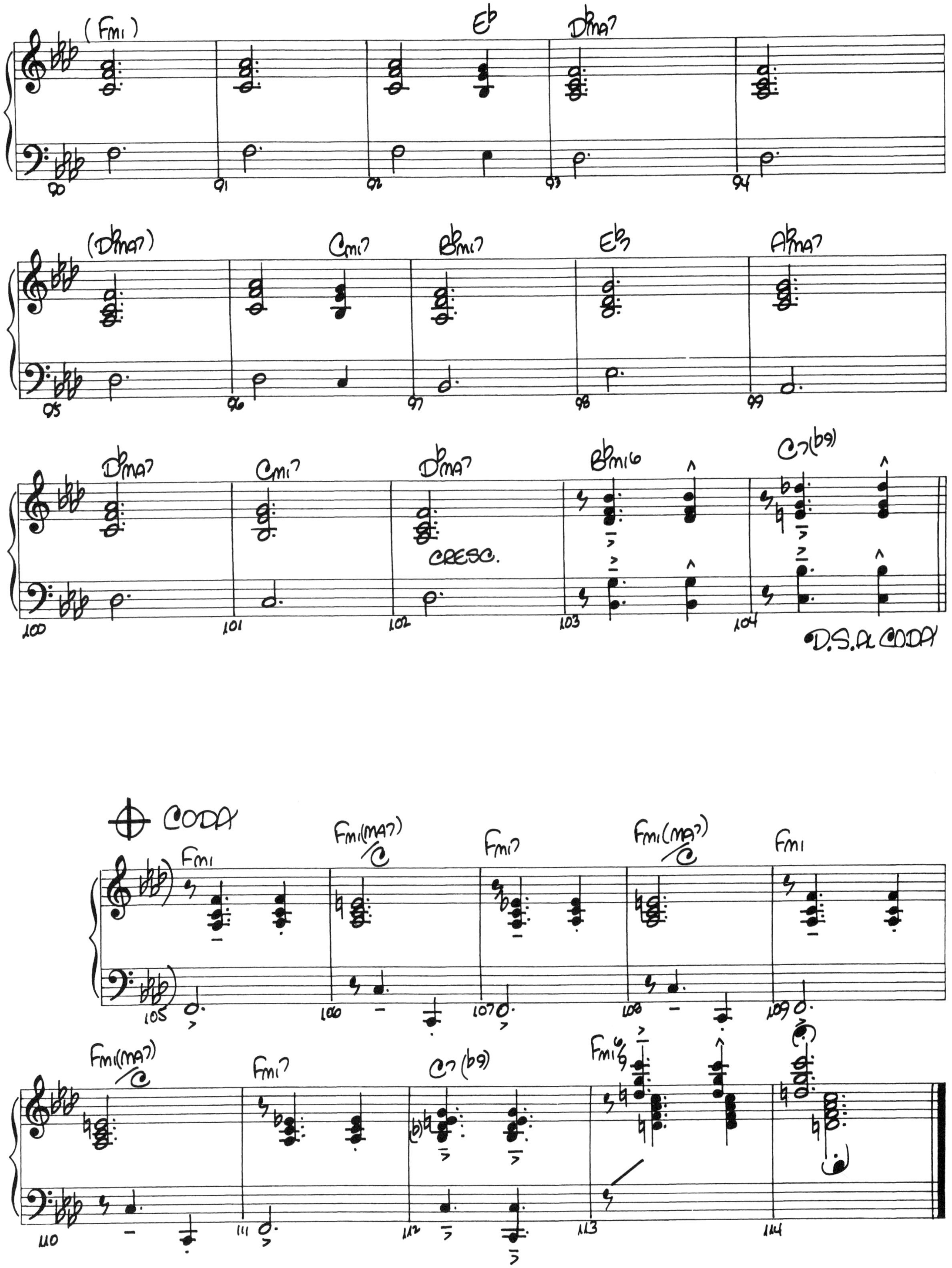
(Fmi)
Eb
DbMA7
(DbMA7)
Cmi7
Bbmi7
Eb7
AbMA7
DbMA7
Cmi7
DbMA7
CRESC.
Bbmi6
C7(b9)
D.S. AL CODA
CODA
Fmi
Fmi(MA7)/C
Fmi7
Fmi(MA7)/C
Fmi
Fmi(MA7)/C
Fmi7
C7(b9)
Fmi6/9

THIS PAGE HAS BEEN LEFT BLANK TO ACCOMMODATE PAGE TURNS.

From the Paramount Picture THE LEMON DROP KID

SILVER BELLS

Words and Music by
JAY LIVINGSTON and RAY EVANS
Arranged by GEORGE STONE

PIANO

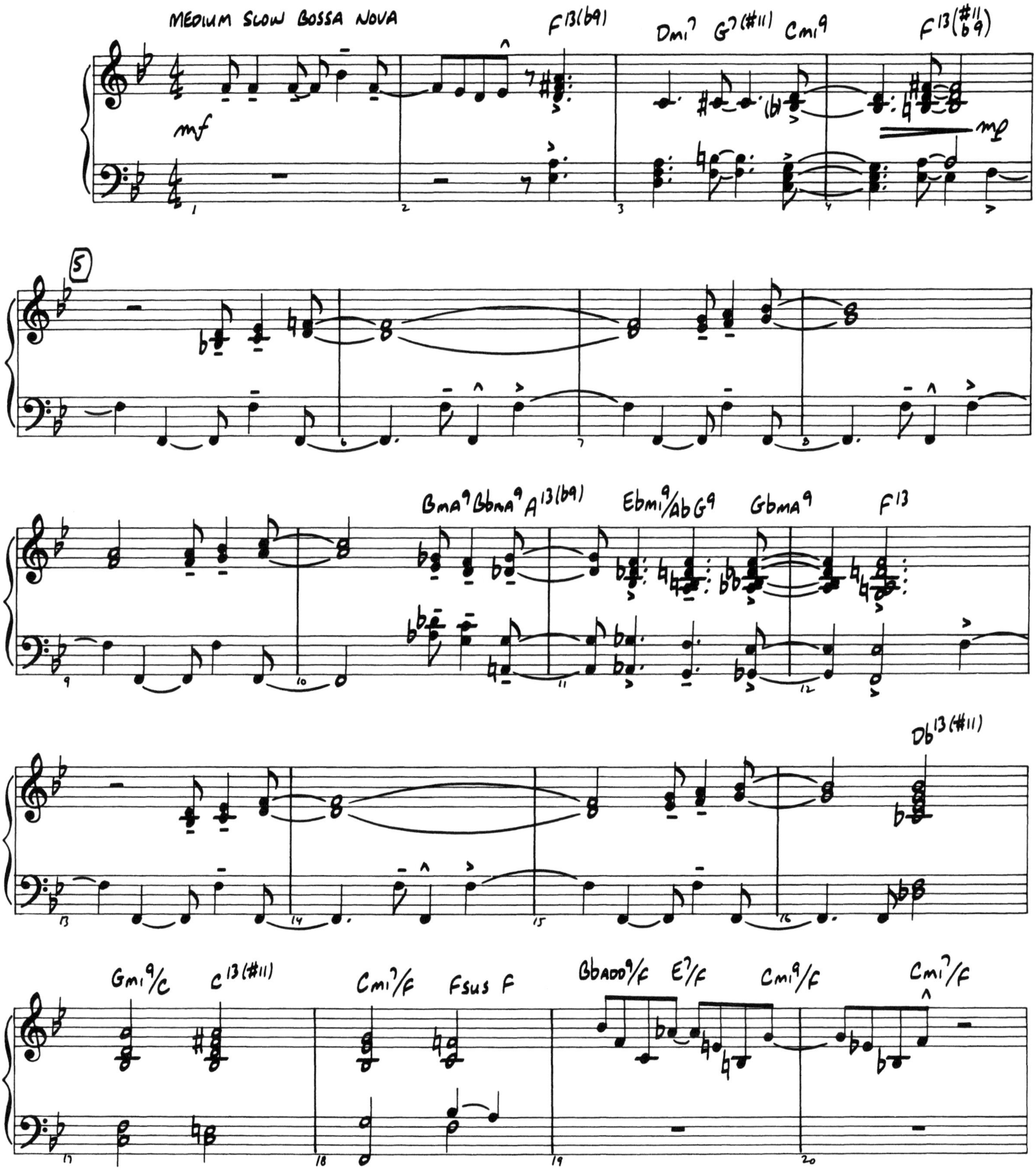

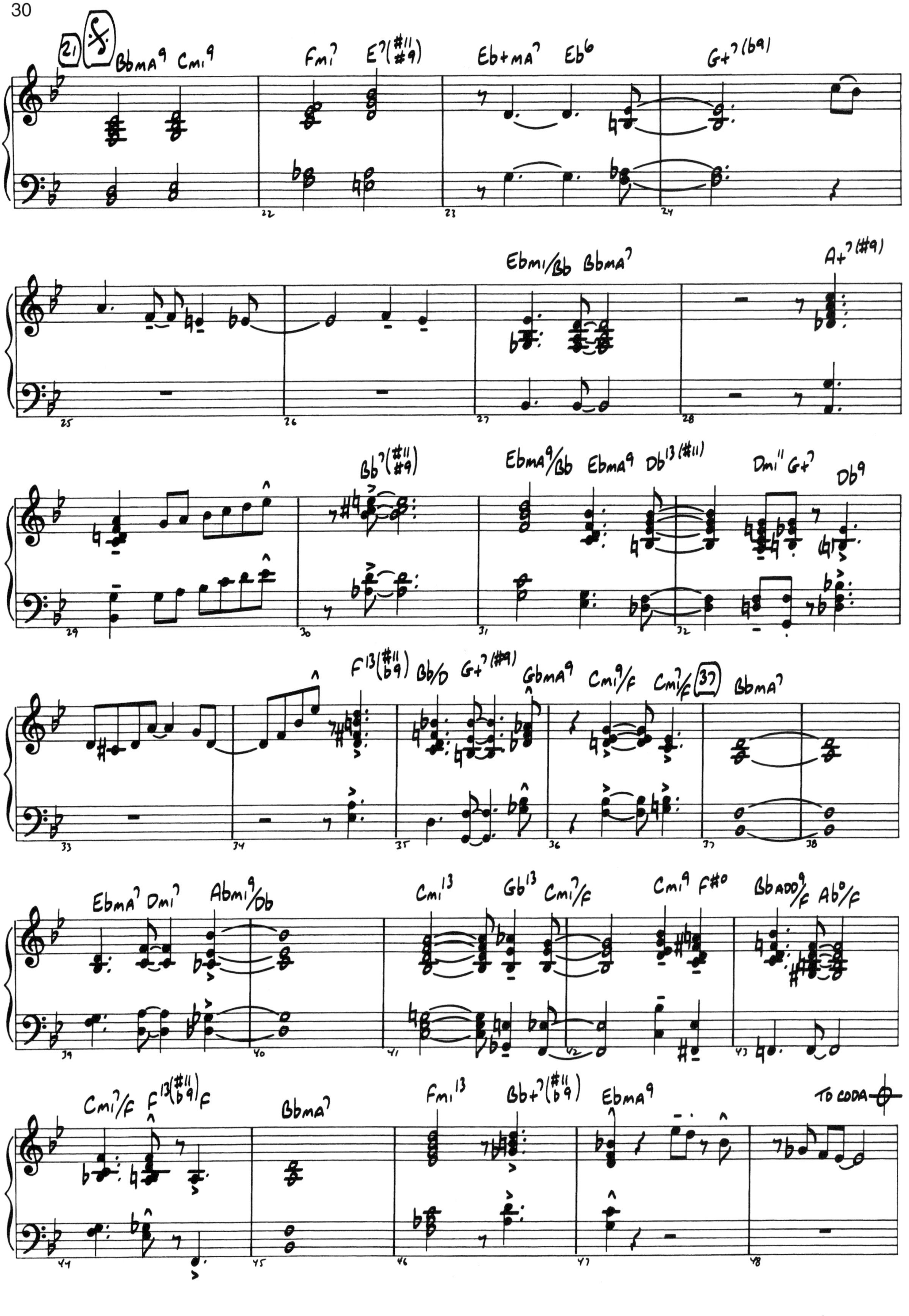
21
BbmA9 Cmi9
Fmi7 E7(#11 #9)
Eb+mA7 Eb6
G+7(b9)
Ebmi/Bb BbmA7
A+7(#9)
Bb7(#11 #9)
EbmA9/Bb EbmA9 Db13(#11)
Dmi11 G+7
Db9
F13(#11 b9) Bb/D G+7(#9)
GbmA9
Cmi9/F
Cmi7/F
37
BbmA7
EbmA7 Dmi7
Abmi9/Db
Cmi13
Gb13 Cmi7/F
Cmi9 F#0
BbADD9/F Ab0/F
Cmi7/F F13(#11 b9)F
BbmA7
Fmi13
Bb+7(#11 b9)
EbmA9
TO CODA

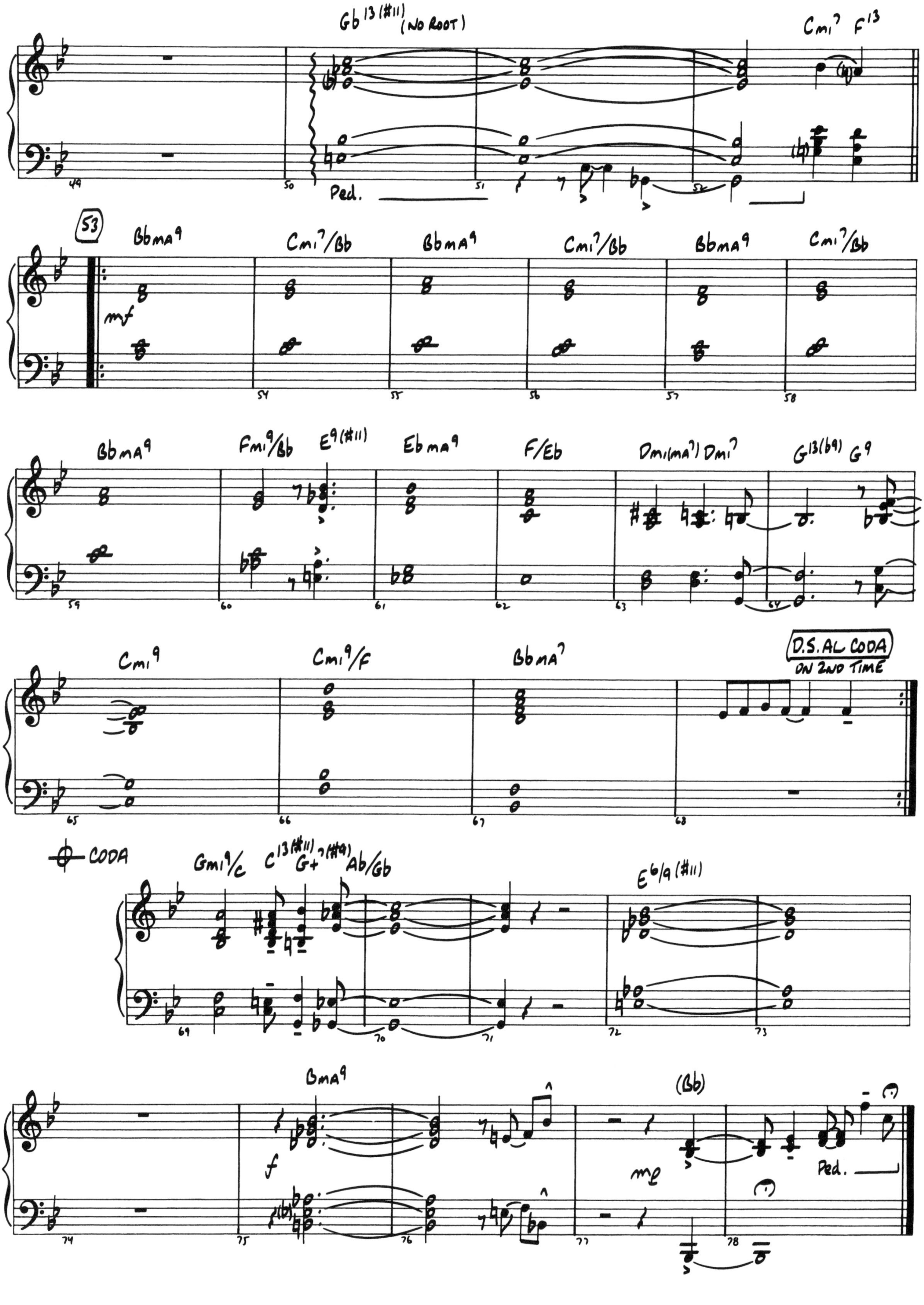
Gb13(#11) (NO ROOT)
Cmi7 F13
Ped.
53
Bbma9
Cmi7/Bb
mf
Fmi9/Bb
E9(#11)
Ebma9
F/Eb
Dmi(ma7) Dmi7
G13(b9) G9
Cmi9
Cmi9/F
Bbma7
D.S. AL CODA
ON 2ND TIME
CODA
Gmi9/C
Ab/Gb
E6/9(#11)
Bma9
f
(Bb)
mp
Ped.

THIS CHRISTMAS

PIANO

Words and Music by
DONNY HATHAWAY and NADINE McKINNOR
Arranged by JOHN BERRY

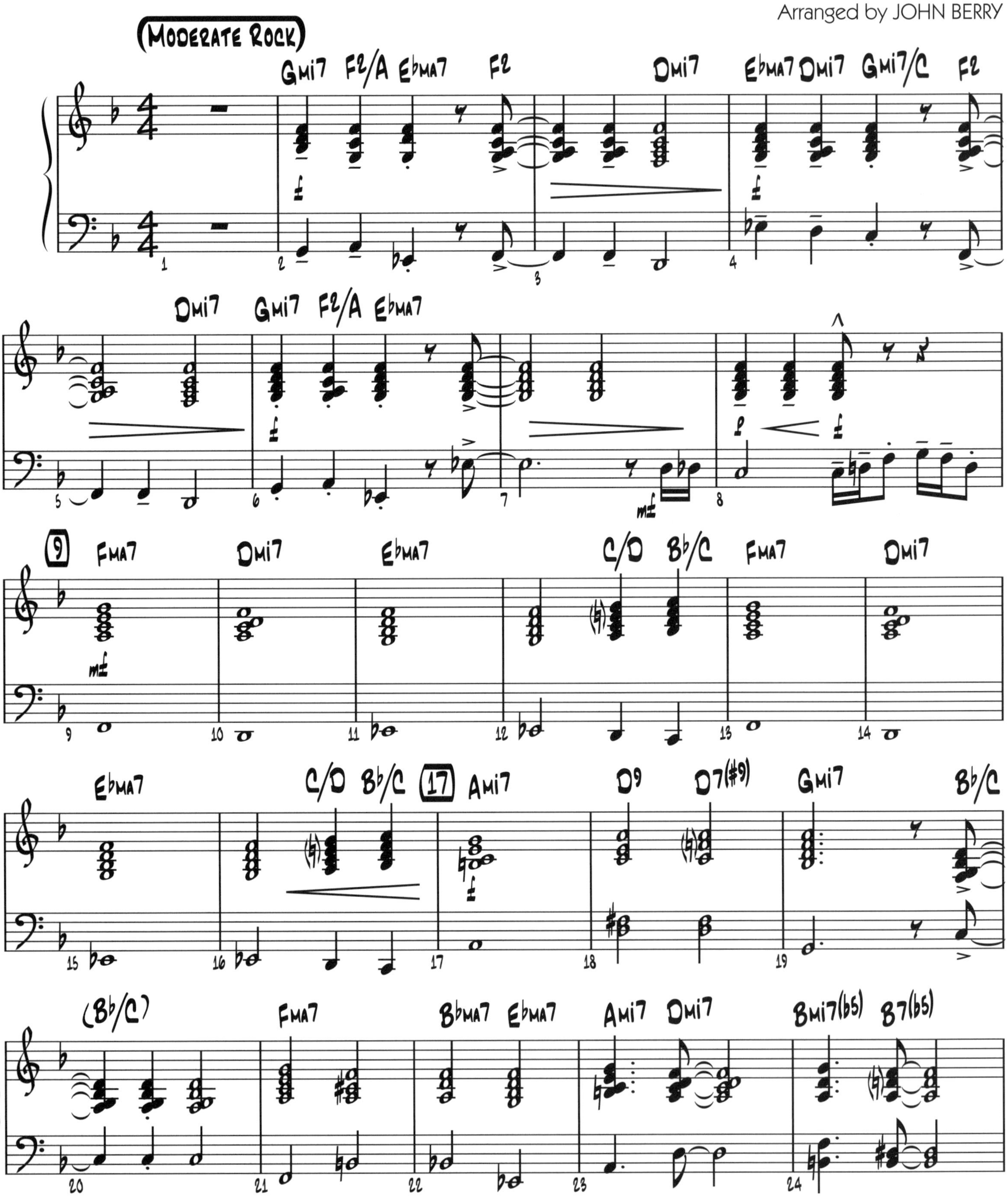

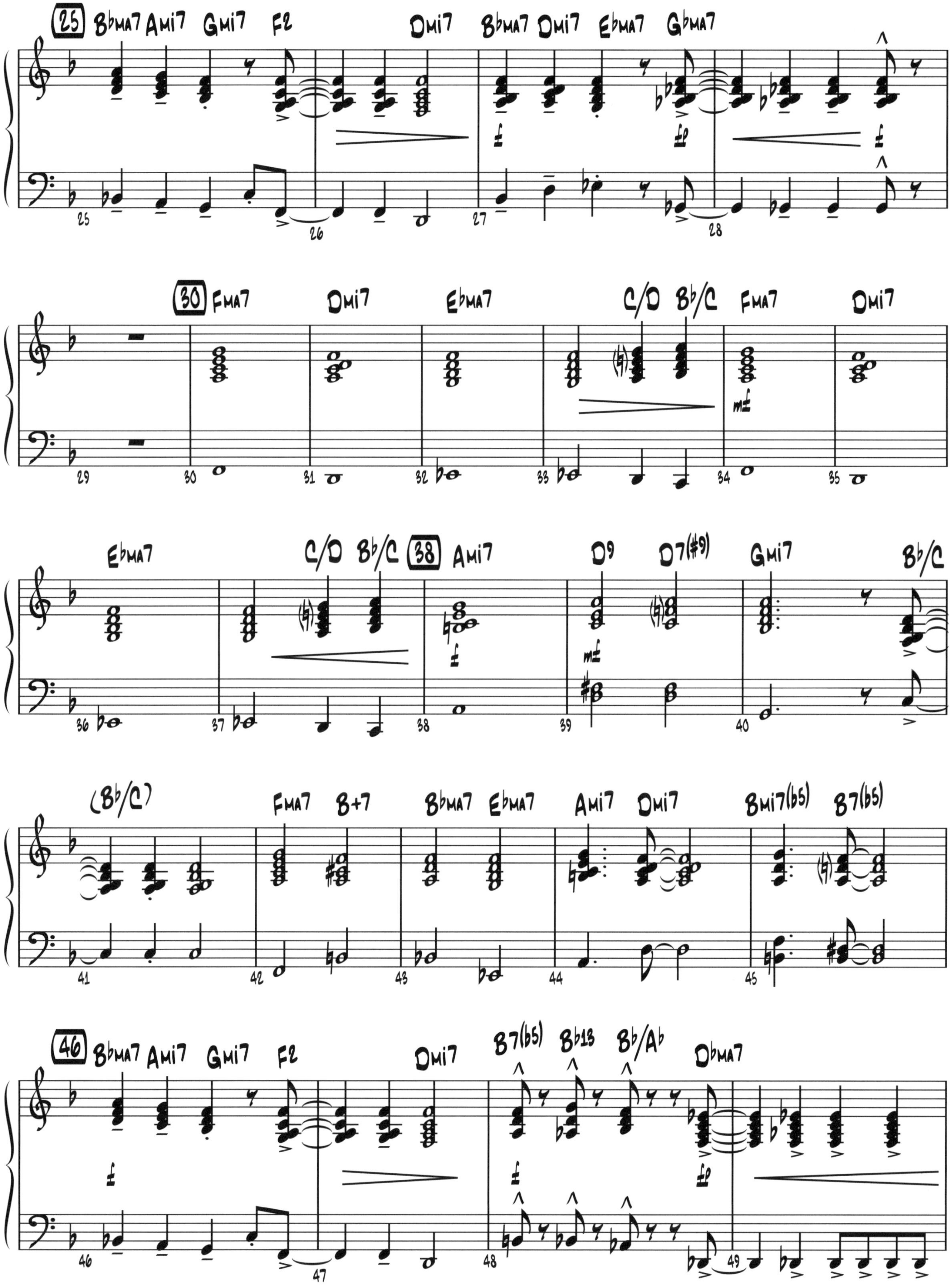
25 B♭MA7 AMI7 GMI7 F2 DMI7 B♭MA7 DMI7 E♭MA7 G♭MA7
30 FMA7 DMI7 E♭MA7 C/D B♭/C FMA7 DMI7
E♭MA7 C/D B♭/C 38 AMI7 D9 D7(♯9) GMI7 B♭/C
(B♭/C) FMA7 B+7 B♭MA7 E♭MA7 AMI7 DMI7 BMI7(♭5) B7(♭5)
46 B♭MA7 AMI7 GMI7 F2 DMI7 B7(♭5) B♭13 B♭/A♭ D♭MA7

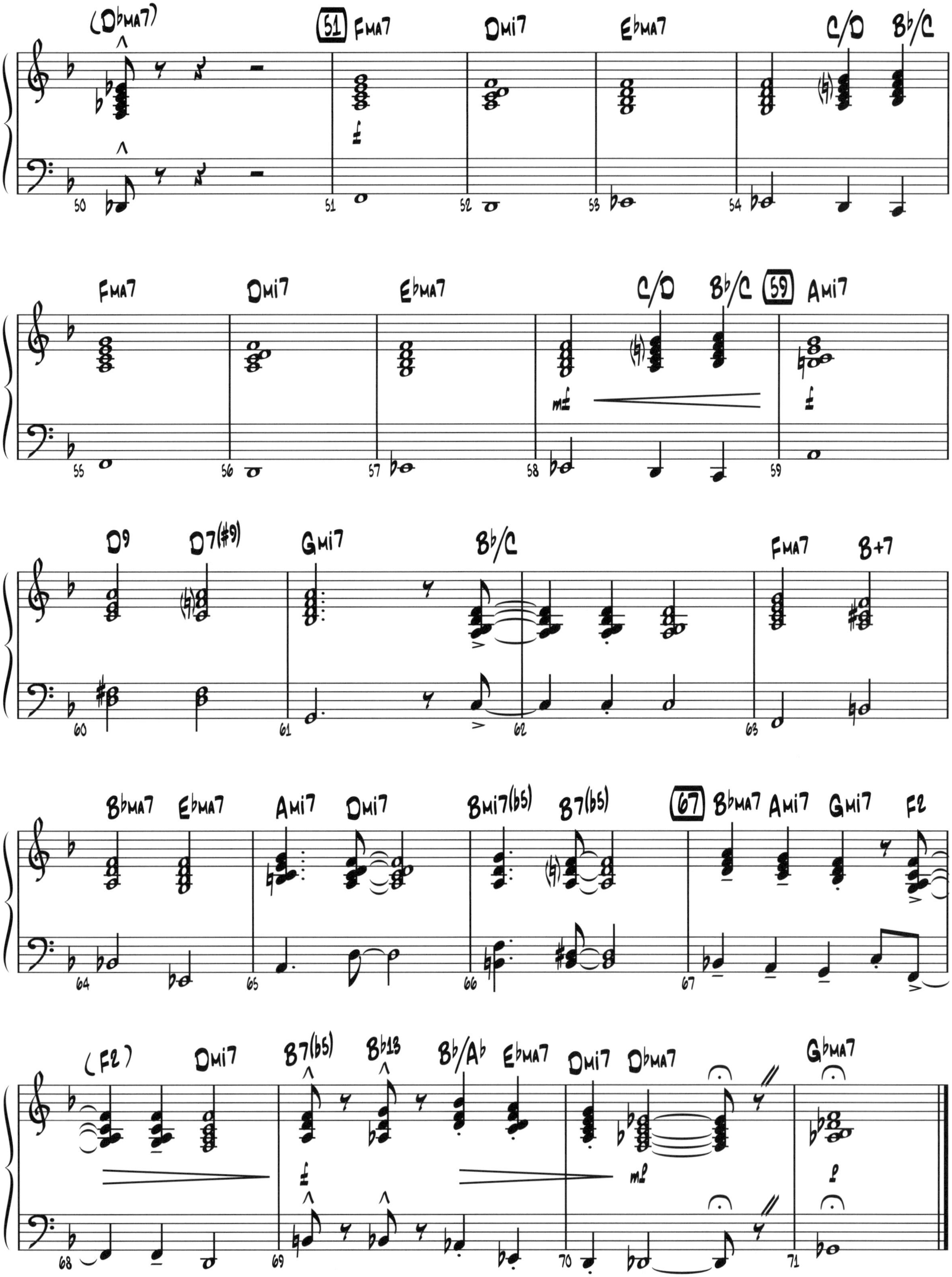
(D♭MA7)
51 FMA7
DMI7
E♭MA7
C/D
B♭/C
FMA7
DMI7
E♭MA7
C/D
B♭/C
59 AMI7
mf
f
D9
D7(♯9)
GMI7
B♭/C
FMA7
B+7
B♭MA7
E♭MA7
AMI7
DMI7
BMI7(♭5)
B7(♭5)
67 B♭MA7
AMI7
GMI7
F2
(F2)
DMI7
B7(♭5)
B♭13
B♭/A♭
E♭MA7
DMI7
D♭MA7
G♭MA7
f
mp
p

From the Motion Picture Irving Berlin's **HOLIDAY INN**

WHITE CHRISTMAS

PIANO

Words and Music by
IRVING BERLIN
Arranged by PAUL JENNINGS

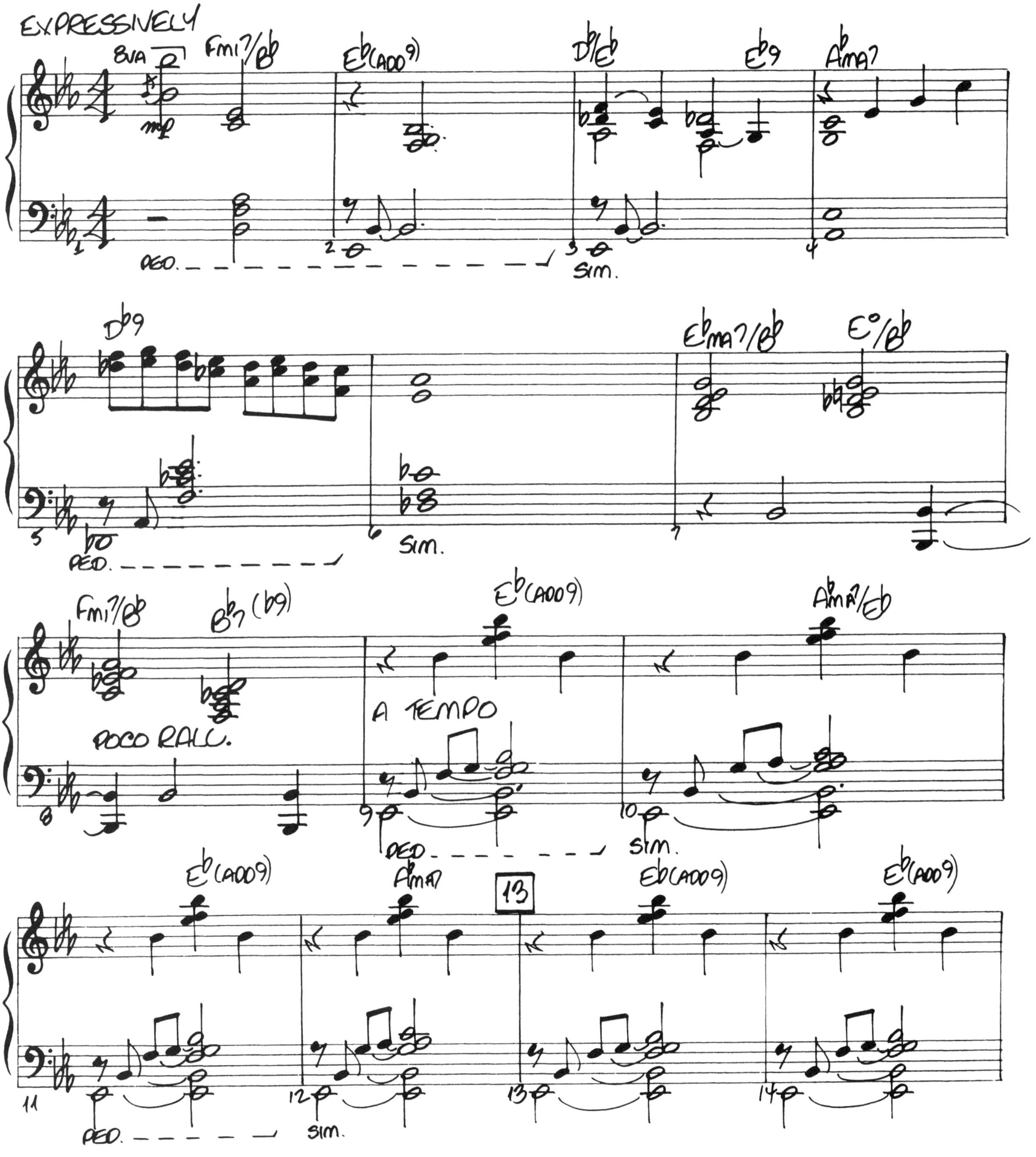

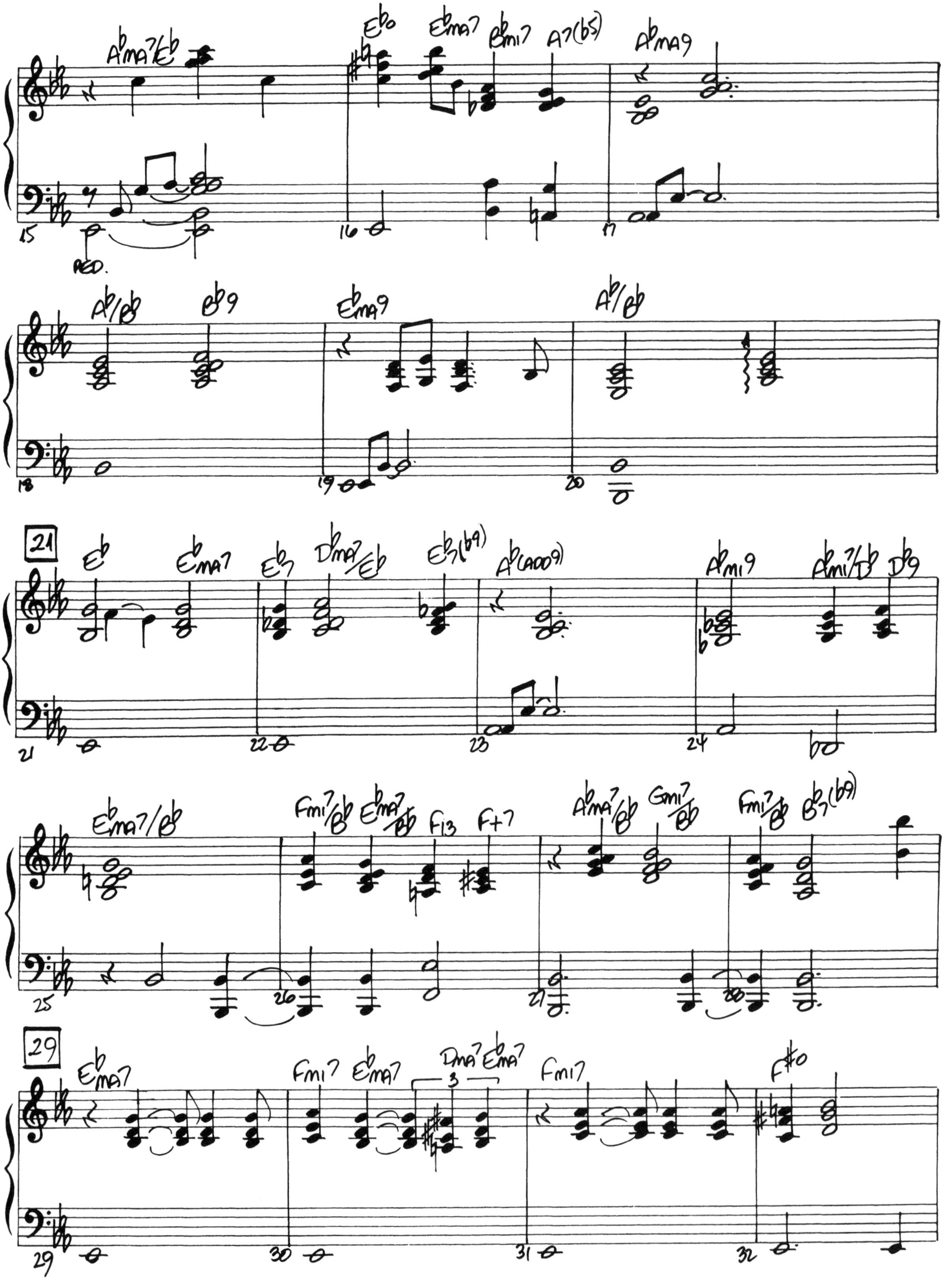
A♭MA7/E♭
E♭o
E♭MA7
B♭MI7
A7(♭5)
A♭MA9
PED.
A♭/B♭
B♭9
E♭MA9
A♭/B♭
21
E♭
E♭MA7
E♭7
D♭MA7/E♭
E♭7(♭9)
A♭(ADD9)
A♭MI9
A♭MI7/D♭
D♭9
E♭MA7/B♭
FMI7/B♭
E♭MA7/B♭
F13
F+7
A♭MA7/B♭
GMI7/B♭
FMI7/B♭
B♭7(♭9)
29
E♭MA7
FMI7
E♭MA7
3
DMA7
E♭MA7
FMI7
F♯o

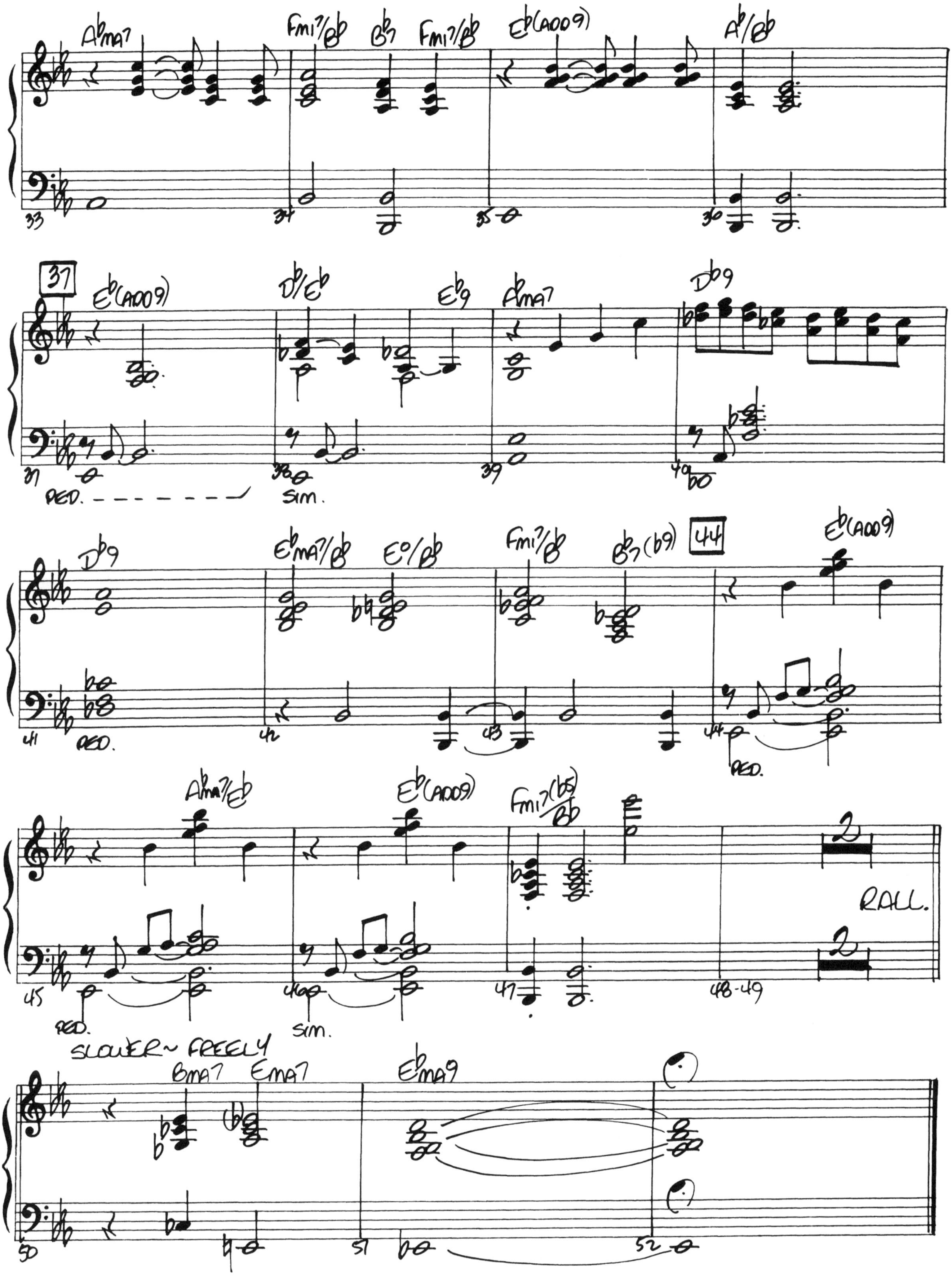
A♭MA7
Fmi7/B♭
B♭7
Fmi7/B♭
E♭(ADD9)
A♭/B♭
33
34
35
36
37
E♭(ADD9)
D♭/E♭
E♭9
A♭MA7
D♭9
PED.
SIM.
38
39
40
D♭9
E♭MA7/B♭
E°/B♭
Fmi7/B♭
B♭7(♭9)
44
E♭(ADD9)
41
PED.
42
43
PED.
A♭MA7/E♭
E♭(ADD9)
Fmi7(♭5)/B♭
2
RALL.
45
PED.
46
SIM.
47
48-49
SLOWER~FREELY
BMA7
EMA7
E♭MA9
50
51
52

THE BIG BAND PLAY-ALONG SERIES

CD INCLUDED

HAL•LEONARD
BIG BAND PLAY-ALONG

These revolutionary play-along packs are great products for those who want a big band sound to back up their instrument, without the pressure of playing solo. They're perfect for current players and for those former players who want to get back in the swing!

Each volume includes:

- Easy-to-read, authentic big band arrangements
- Professional recordings on CD of all the big band instruments, including the lead part
- Editions for alto sax, tenor sax, trumpet, trombone, guitar, piano, bass, and drums

1. SWING FAVORITES

April in Paris • I've Got You Under My Skin • In the Mood • It Don't Mean a Thing (If It Ain't Got That Swing) • Route 66 • Speak Low • Stompin' at the Savoy • Tangerine • This Can't Be Love • Until I Met You (Corner Pocket).

07011313	Alto Sax	$14.95
07011314	Tenor Sax	$14.95
07011315	Trumpet	$14.95
07011316	Trombone	$14.95
07011317	Guitar	$14.95
07011318	Piano	$14.95
07011319	Bass	$14.95
07011320	Drums	$14.95

2. POPULAR HITS

Ain't No Mountain High Enough • Brick House • Copacabana (At the Copa) • Evil Ways • I Heard It Through the Grapevine • On Broadway • Respect • Street Life • Yesterday • Zoot Suit Riot.

07011321	Alto Sax	$14.95
07011322	Tenor Sax	$14.95
07011323	Trumpet	$14.95
07011324	Trombone	$14.95
07011325	Guitar	$14.95
07011326	Piano	$14.95
07011327	Bass	$14.95
07011328	Drums	$14.95

3. DUKE ELLINGTON

Caravan • Chelsea Bridge • Cotton Tail • I'm Beginning to See the Light • I'm Just a Lucky So and So • In a Mellow Tone • In a Sentimental Mood • Mood Indigo • Satin Doll • Take the "A" Train.

00843086	Alto Sax	$14.95
00843087	Tenor Sax	$14.95
00843088	Trumpet	$14.95
00843089	Trombone	$14.95
00843090	Guitar	$14.95
00843091	Piano	$14.95
00843092	Bass	$14.95
00843093	Drums	$14.95

4. JAZZ CLASSICS

Bags' Groove • Blue 'N Boogie • Blue Train (Blue Trane) • Doxy • Four • Moten Swing • Oleo • Song for My Father • Stolen Moments • Straight No Chaser.

00843094	Alto Sax	$14.95
00843095	Tenor Sax	$14.95
00843096	Trumpet	$14.95
00843097	Trombone	$14.95
00843098	Guitar	$14.95
00843099	Piano	$14.95
00843100	Bass	$14.95
00843101	Drums	$14.95

HAL•LEONARD® CORPORATION
7777 W. BLUEMOUND RD. P.O. BOX 13819 MILWAUKEE, WI 53213

Prices, contents and availability subject to change without notice.

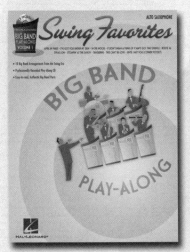

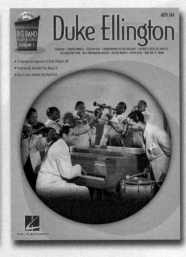

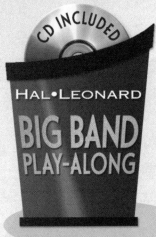

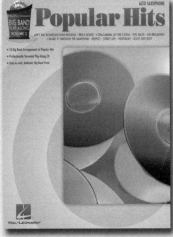

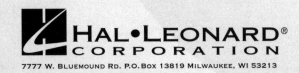

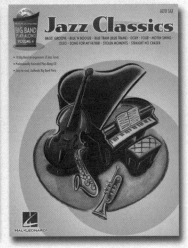

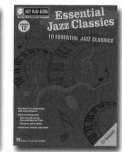

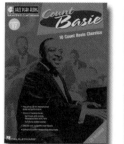

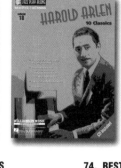

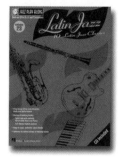

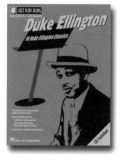

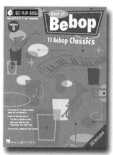